A Parent's Guide™ to
Boston

Kim Foley MacKinnon

Kim Foley MacKi

parent's guide press
Los Angeles, CA
www.pgpress.com

A Parent's Guide™ to
Boston

Text and Maps © Mars Publishing 2002
Photos © Photographers as noted
ISBN: 1-931199-11-6

This book, and all titles in the Parent's Guide series, are available for purposes of fund raising and educational sales to charity drives, fund raisers, parent or teacher organizations, schools, government agencies and corporations at a discount for purchases of more than 10 copies. Persons or organizations wishing to inquire should call Mars Publishing at 1-800-549-6646 or write to us at **sales@marspub.com**.

At the time of publication of this book, all of the information contained within was correct to the best of our knowledge. If you find information in this book that has changed, please contact us. Even better, if you have additional places to recommend, please let us know. Any included submissions to the new edition of this book will get the submitter a by-line in the book and a free copy of any Mars publication.

Please contact us at **parentsguides@marspub.com**

parent's guide press

Edwin E. Steussy, CEO and Publisher
Lars W. Peterson, Project Editor
Michael P. Duggan, Graphic Artist

PO Box 461730
Los Angeles CA 90046

contents

contents

Author's Note

I owe a lot of thanks to a lot of people. Without the support of my family and friends, I never would have been able to finish this book. I had a blast doing research with you all. Your comments, suggestions, and criticism kept me on target. You explored the city with me tirelessly and joyfully. So, thanks again, Elizabeth, Jen B., Jennifer L., Jorge, Karen, Kim, Sarah and everybody else who was cheering me on. Your photos are great, Jen Bester.

Many institutions were very generous with information, time and tickets, and I sincerely appreciate all the assistance given to me. I want to thank Mars Publishing for taking a chance on me. I had a great time and am very grateful for having had the opportunity.

An extra heartfelt thanks to those I live with, Rob, Sadie, and Mom. I'm sure I was unbearable, but you always encouraged and supported me.

One more note of gratitude goes to Leila Saad. Without her thinking of me, the opportunity to write this book never would have come up.

Introduction

I am not a native Bostonian. Loving Boston came slowly to me. I moved here 10 years ago with every expectation of moving on again in a few years. But like many people who think Boston will be a temporary home, I was hooked. Now I can't imagine living anywhere else. Boston seems small and large, old and new, all at once. I never tire of exploring the city, and it never disappoints.

Introduction

Boston is rich in history—the word "first" and "old" before an attraction in this guide will become familiar to you soon. But the city doesn't remain stuck in the past. It can't. With more than 50 colleges and universities in the area, Boston is constantly changing and growing, adding new firsts all the time. Thousands of students keep the city energized, many of them falling in love with Boston, like I did, and making it their home. At the same time it embraces the new, Boston is fiercely attached to its history. We've saved many sites that played an important role in our history, and you'll find them flush against new skyscrapers and office buildings.

As any parent will tell you, having a child makes you look at the world in a different way. I am happy to look at Boston through a different lens. My daughter is lucky to grow up in the city. She takes it for granted that Boston Common and the Public Garden are her personal playgrounds. Her preschool regularly checks books out of the grand Central Boston Public Library (the oldest free public library; the first library with a children's room—see what I mean about "old" and "first"?) in Copley Square. While these seem commonplace to her now, someday she'll know the privilege she had learning in the Hub.

I hope this book conveys the excitement and adventure Boston holds for us and for anyone, especially families, willing to open their eyes to all that is around them.

About This Guide

Boston's newest bridge, the Leonard P. Zakim Bunker Hill Bridge, is a beautiful addition to the skyline.

Like many metropolitan areas, Boston is a series of little neighborhoods. It is called "America's Walking City" with good reason—it's much easier to walk than drive in any one area. It makes sense then to organize this book by neighborhood, rather than by activities or categories that might send you back and forth across town, wasting precious vacation time and trying your kids' patience. Within each neighborhood, venues are given

Introduction

Greater
Boston

North
West◀●▶East
South

CAMBRIDGE

CHARLESTOWN

SOMERVILLE

CHARLESTOWN
(Chap 2)

NORTH
END
(Chap 2)

CAMBRIDGE/
HARVARD
SQUARE
(Chap 2)

BEACON
HILL
(Chap 2)

DOWNTOWN
& WATERFRONT
(Chap 2)

FENWAY
(Chap 2)

BACK
BAY
(Chap 2)

BOSTON

BROOKLINE

JAMAICA
PLAIN

DORCHESTER

ROXBURY

in alphabetical order. At the end of every section, I've listed the area's best play-ground for when the kids' just need to run around and be loud. An outdoor break, even if lasts just for 15 minutes, can buy you time later at a museum or restaurant. Chapter One gives a quick orientation to the city and how to get around. Chapter Two is where you'll find the bulk of local activities. Driving in Boston is an art form—one not practiced successfully by many natives. Whenever practical, I've given directions using public transportation. If you are driving, be prepared to get lost, but don't panic. Boston isn't that big.

Introduction

One thing Boston has is a surplus of walking trails and tours. Everyone has heard of the Freedom Trail, but what about the Black Heritage Trail? Or the Literary Trail? Chapter Three details the best and most interesting ones of the lot. Whether you go on your own or opt for a guided tour, taking in the city this way is a great orientation. Since going to the theatre or a symphony are more planned events than something you do while sightseeing, I've put them by themselves, in Chapter Four. Almost every higher cultural institution in Boston schedules special family- or child-oriented events. To give a comprehensive listing of hotels and restaurants would be beyond the scope of this book, but I have listed a few that are super family-friendly. Not everyone knows where you can have Sunday brunch in your pajamas or where parents can eat gourmet meals while the kids play within sight in an activity area set up just for them. Chapter Five covers the top picks in the city.

www.nps.gov

Many venues in the Boston area are run by the National Park Service, and you'll find lots of valuable information at their website.

There are many places within an easy drive or train ride from Boston, which you'll find in Chapter Six. Even those with limited time in Boston will find most of them convenient. I've offered a couple of itineraries for those who want help planning a short stay or need ideas for a weekend in town in Chapter Seven. Martha's Vineyard and Nantucket are also covered in Chapter Seven. You'll need at least a weekend to visit the popular islands, so you'll find a couple of suggestions for where to stay and eat, too. Finally, the Appendix has a calendar of events, important phone numbers and websites, and how to find discounts and deals.

I should note that with Boston's rich history, museums are to be found at every turn. Higher cultural institutions aren't always the most exciting of visits for many kids, especially little ones (unless it's the Children's Museum, of course). Therefore, where I could, I included details of any programs the museums offer. Some have re-enactments, or crafts days; some have story hours. I think these are great ways to get kids interested and enthusiastic about museums. Many have family activity packs. Be sure to ask. I did not limit the guide to any specific age group. Where appropriate, I've noted whether teenagers or toddlers would be more interested, but hopefully, most sites will interest the whole family.

1

All About Boston

History

Beantown. Hub of the Solar System. Athens of America. City on a Hill. America's Walking City. The Cradle of Liberty. Boston is called many things, but not one of them can quite capture all that it is. It is impossible to ignore Boston's more than 350 years of history. We're drenched in it. The Freedom Trail offers a take on some of the more historic sites, but it's only the tip of the iceberg.

All About Boston

Boston is a city that was created improbably by landfills. Back Bay, now a highly desirable part of town, was once a smelly mudflat. The project to fill it in during the late-1800s almost doubled the city's size. Actually, man, rather than nature, designed a lot of Boston's landscape. The North End and Charles Street were also mudflats. They were filled in with dirt from what was once Trimountaine, three hills where Beacon Hill alone remains. The State House is as tall as Beacon Hill itself once was. The Emerald Necklace, a chain of public parks designed by Frederick Law Olmsted, was another partial solution to the mudflat problem.

Most people know Boston's place in America's history. Here's a short overview. Boston started as a colony in 1630, when John Winthrop and other Puritans settled here with a charter from England. Two years later, Boston was the capital of the Massachusetts Bay Colony. (The name "Massachusetts" comes from the Native Americans who originally settled here years earlier. They were pretty much wiped out by European epidemics.) In 1684, Britain revoked the charter, but granted a new one in 1691. In 1765, things started to heat up in response to the Stamp Act, which required payment to England for any kind of business transaction. This was a short-lived act. The colony resented Britain's unfair policies, including taxation and the Writs of Assistance (search warrants). Five years later, the "Boston Massacre" occurred, during which British troops killed five colonists in front of the Old State House, and the population of the city was inflamed. In 1773, the Sons of Liberty dumped 342 crates of tea in the harbor, a protest forever after remembered as the "Boston Tea Party." Finally, things came to a head in 1775, when the British invaded and the American Revolution began.

After the Revolutionary War, Boston got back down to the business of making itself a city of firsts. The first church in the nation built by free blacks opened. The country's first abolitionist newspaper was published. The nation's first free library opened. Other firsts for Boston include the country's first telephone and the first subway system. The list goes on and on, and Boston adds to it all the time.

All About Boston

Orientation

The main neighborhoods of the city—Beacon Hill, Back Bay, Downtown, the Waterfront, Chinatown, the North End, and the South End are very accessible to each other. They each have a distinct character, but there is no real demarcation line among any of them. In the middle of all these neighborhoods are Boston Common and the Public Garden, two of the city's best public spaces, separated only by Charles Street. The streets downtown, rather than following any logical order, instead follow the old routes of days gone by. The one-way streets, dead-ends, and random turns make sense only if you're on foot. For drivers, they are just a hassle. Whenever I can, I take public transportation downtown to save myself heaps of frustration. A little farther afield, but still accessible by the subway, are the Fenway, Charlestown, Brookline, Jamaica Plain, Dorchester, and Roxbury. Look at the map to get a feel for the locations. Across the Charles River is Cambridge and Harvard Square, also easily accessed by subway.

> We have long street names that we get tired of saying, so we shorten them. In fact, we don't like to use the complete name for anything. Here's a translation of two streets in case you ask somebody for directions and they tell you to go down Comm. Ave., past the Dunkin' Donuts, or take a right on Mass. Ave. at the Dunkin' Donuts. (One thing about Boston, all directions are given in relation to where the Dunkin' Donuts is; there are dozens in Boston.) Comm. Ave.= Commonwealth Avenue; Mass. Ave.= Massachusetts Avenue. Oh, we shorten building names, too. The "Pru" is short for the Prudential Building; the BPL is the main library; BC is Boston College, not to be confused with BU, Boston University.

Getting Here
By Air

Most people fly into Logan International Airport (800)23-LOGAN; **www.massport.com**), which is two miles from town. Public transportation, via subway, bus or boat, makes getting into the city easy. A free shuttle operates between the airport and the MBTA subway (referred to as the "T"), where you can ride the Blue Line downtown and transfer to where you need to go. Cabs are plentiful. Fares start at $1.50 and cost $.20 per 1/7 mile after that. Add a buck for rides from the airport (the passenger is also responsible for tolls). A fun way to get from the airport to the city, or vice versa, is the Airport Water Shuttle. It takes only seven minutes from the airport to Rowes Wharf. You can catch a free shuttle to the dock at any terminal. Roundtrip is $17; one-way costs $10; under 12, free. Call (617) 330-8680.

All About Boston

By Train

Amtrak pulls into the North, South and Back Bay stations, (800) 872-7245; **www.amtrak.com**. South Station, located at Atlantic Avenue and Summer Street, is the main terminal. You can easily catch a cab or take the subway from here to any downtown hotel.

Getting Around

Driving in Boston

There is really no reason to drive in Boston, especially downtown. Unless, of course, you enjoy terrible traffic, circling like a vulture for parking spaces, and either yelling or being yelled at. Too many cars, not enough space. That's it in a nutshell. Zipcars (cars you can "buy into," sort of like a timeshare vacation condo) are becoming very popular here because many people don't think it's worthwhile to own a car. Walk or take public transportation if you can. Plus, children always think subways are an adventure in and of themselves. The destination hardly matters. I wouldn't be lying if I said I've ridden the train with my daughter back and forth just because she enjoyed it. My advice, if you are from out of town and have a car, is to use parking garages. They are expensive, but they are plentiful and convenient.

Factor high parking fees ($20 a day is not unusual) into your vacation budget and save yourself a lot of stress. See if you can find an all-day lot, leave the car there, and pick it up at the end of the day. If you are jumping around the city, it is still more prudent to leave the car in one spot and use the subway.

So, now you've been warned. Sometimes though, you just gotta drive. Rotaries are a painful part of driving in Boston. In theory, the driver already in the roundabout has right of way. In reality, Boston's traffic circles are a free-for-all; whoever is the pushiest, wins. It seems to me every time that I am in one, I am risking life and limb. Don't assume anyone is going to yield to you.

Top Five Reasons Not to Drive in Boston

1 **Apparently missing street signs.** That's right. Many streets don't have signs. This is on purpose, not an accident.

2 **Roads change daily.** I mean this literally. One day a road is there. The next day, it's gone or goes in a new direction. This is thanks to the Big Dig (more info below).

3 **Pedestrians do not obey traffic laws.** They will dart in front of your car, out of nowhere.

4 **Drivers do not obey traffic laws.** They will run lights. They will tailgate. Oh, and they rarely use signals.

5 **Finally, you will double all your expenses by paying exorbitant parking fees if you insist on driving.** Or, if you luck out and find a parking space, you'll end up feeding the meter or getting a ticket when you are delayed trying to get change somewhere.

All About Boston

Public Transportation

The 'T' and Railways around Boston

North
West ◀●▶ East
South

Oak Grove

Wonderland

Sullivan Square

Alewife

Lochmere

North Station

Bowdoin

Haymarket

Airport

Boston College

Park St

State

Kenmore

Copley

Downtown Crossing

Riverside

Cleveland Circle

South Station

Heath

JFK/ UMass

Forest Hills

Mattapan

Braintree

Red Line ▭▭▭
Green Line ▬▬▬
Orange Line ▭▭▭
Blue Line ≣≣≣

Commuter Rails – – –

All About Boston

By far the best way to get around town, other than your own two feet, is the "T," short for the Massachusetts Bay Transportation Authority (MBTA). The T is America's oldest subway line and the fourth largest in the country. It goes almost everywhere you want to go. There are four main subway lines that go downtown and out to various neighborhoods. When people talk about the T, they usually are referring to the train service, but the MBTA also runs buses and commuter trains.

Riding the T can be a little confusing for newcomers. If you remember that "Inbound" trains head toward the Park Street Station (the heart of the city) and "Outbound" trains head away from Park Street, you should be okay. To add to your confusion, although there are four colors of trains, some of them have more than one line. For example, the Green line has "B," "C," and "D" trains. Get a map and don't be afraid to ask for help!

But Mom, why is it called the Green Line? Facts kids want to know.

The Green Line was the first subway in America. It went from Park Street to Boylston Street in 1897. It's called the Green Line because it travels through the Emerald Necklace (details on this later).

The Red Line is called "Red" because it used to end at Harvard University, whose school color is crimson.

The Blue Line is so-called because it was the first subway in the world to travel under the ocean.

The Orange Line runs down Washington Street, which used to be named Orange Way.

The subway fare is $1 for adults; half-price for kids 5-11; and free for kids under 5. A great deal is the "Visitor Passport." You can buy an unlimited travel pass for one day ($6); three days, ($11); or seven days ($22). This pass is good for train and bus service. Call the MBTA at (617) 222-3200 for more info and to order your passes in advance, or visit their website at www.mbta.com. Another bargain is the "Commuter Rail Family Fare." Five people, consisting of either one adult and four children, or two adults and three children, can ride for the price of two adult round-trip tickets (off-peak). The price varies depending on the destination. This makes day-trips a little cheaper for families.

All About Boston

Exploring on Foot

Check on Boston weather by looking at the (old) John Hancock's weather lights on top of the building. Just memorize this little ditty, well-known to all Boston city school children. Don't know where to look? The newer 60-story Hancock building dominates the skyline. The old one nearby is reflected in its mirror-like windows.

Steady Blue, clear view.

Flashing Blue, clouds due.

Steady red, rain ahead.

Flashing red, snow instead (except in the summer, when flashing red means the Red Sox game is cancelled).

Walking is absolutely the best way to experience Boston. Of course, sometimes those little short people traveling with you don't like to walk. If practical, bring a kiddie backpack. Lots of stairs make negotiating Boston with a stroller tricky sometimes. If you are sightseeing downtown, you're never far from a subway station. Don't assume that if you are in a crosswalk, cars will stop for you. Crosswalks are more of a suggestion than anything else. Bostonians like to creep up to the light so they can race away when it turns green. If the red and yellow lights are on at a traffic signal, this indicates that pedestrians can cross. Follow your own advice to your kids, and look both ways. Twice.

The Big Dig

Ah, the project Bostonians love to hate, otherwise know as the "Big Dig." This is another good reason to park the car somewhere and find your way on foot or train. The Central Artery/Tunnel Project (its official name), which started in 1995 and will not be completed until around 2004, is costing millions and millions of dollars. It's America's largest public highway project to date. The main elements involve replacing Interstate 93 with an 8-to-10-lane highway tunnel under the city and extending Interstate I-90 (Mass Turnpike) to Logan Airport.

Jennifer Bester

Bostonians can't wait for the Big Dig to be finished.

All About Boston

The incredibly complex project (much condensed here) will result in 150 acres of new parks and open spaces. But so far it has resulted only in daily disruptions of traffic. Detours and road closings are to be expected every hour of the day, seven days a week. Visit **www.bigdig.com** for the latest traffic patterns. While adults may bemoan the project and the hassles it causes, children love it. Counting cranes and backhoes should keep any kid busy. See Chapter Three, Trails & Tours, for a self-guided tour of the Big Dig for really gung-ho construction lovers.

What to Pack

No matter what time of year you visit, you should be prepared for anything. Snow in April, hot summery weather in October, rain one minute, gorgeous sunshine the next. None of that is unusual for Boston. You've heard it before, I'm sure, but dressing in layers is the way to go. Pack some lightweight raincoats that you can put in the bottom of your bag and hopefully never use. A sweater or sweatshirt is essential, even in summer, for those walks along the harbor or in air-conditioned museums. You'll want good, sturdy shoes for exploring cobbled streets.

> **NOT FROM BOSTON:** What are Evacuation Day, Patriots' Day, and Bunker Hill Day anyway? They are all either state or Boston holidays. Cynics might say they are holidays so everyone can participate in or watch the St. Patrick's Day parade (Evacuation Day, celebrates when the British were Evacuated out of Boston in 1776, coincidentally on March 17) and the Boston Marathon (Patriots' Day, 3rd Monday in April, which commemorates the battles of Lexington and Concord which began April 19, 1775), but I'd never put that forth. We are just very patriotic around here. Bunker Hill Day (celebrated Friday closest to June 17) commemorates the Battle of Bunker Hill (which really occurred at Breed's Hill—don't ask, more on this later).

Climate

As mentioned above, the weather in Boston is forever changing. There is no average temperature here, no matter what the weather forecasters say. In the summer, the temperature ranges from 70 to 90 degrees. Fall is anywhere between 50 to 70 degrees, and winter reaches the freezing point and often dips below. Fortunately, it doesn't matter what the weather is, since there's plenty to do and see even on a cold, rainy day. You'll never run out of indoor activities in Boston. If you can shelve expectations and be flexible about outdoor plans, you'll be fine.

2 Boston by Neighborhood

Each of the following neighborhoods has its own distinct character and charms. Beacon Hill, with its old-world Brahmin feel, is where most tourists start their visit. The Boston Common and the State House are familiar landmarks. The Back Bay with its graceful homes and the Public Garden and Copley Square are urban meccas. The John Hancock Tower soars over the area and it's mirror-like windows reflect beautiful Trinity Church and the Boston Public Library. Nearby South End is famous as the largest neighborhood of Victorian homes in the country. While adults might find this fascinating, kids may not. You might head over here for lunch or dinner at one of the many restaurants. Downtown and the Waterfront area beckon with trips out on Boston Harbor and many historic sites. Shoppers can choose between touristy Fanueil Hall, or go to where the locals shop, Filene's Basement in Downtown Crossing. The Fenway area, of course, is home to Fenway Park and the Boston Red Sox. Many of Boston's finest cultural institutions line the "Avenue of the Arts," Huntington Avenue.

Boston by Neighborhood

Anyone with a taste for Italian should head to the North End, Boston's oldest neighborhood. Packed with restaurants, cafés, and locals speaking Italian, you'll forget you're in New England. In Charlestown, "Old Ironsides," the USS *Constitution,* makes its home in the Charlestown Navy Yard. Climbing the Bunker Hill Monument is worth the long climb for its fabulous views. Jamaica Plain, Roxbury, and Dorchester, more on the outskirts of the city, are still an important part of it. Some of the best open space in the city is at the Franklin Park and the Arnold Arboretum. Brookline and Cambridge, their own towns, are close enough to Boston to make all that they have to offer convenient destinations to city residents.

Boston by Neighborhood

Beacon Hill

Beacon Hill, with its cobbled streets, gas lanterns, and Boston Common, is the neighborhood many people see in their mind's eye when thinking about Boston. If it's your first time in the city, you'll probably spend a lot of time here, searching out old historic sites and the meeting places of America's forefathers. The hill, originally called Trimountaine Hill, was too high to build on. In the 1800s, the hill was lowered by carting off dirt to create the Charles Street area and some of the North End, which were mudflats at the time. The other two hills, Pemberton and Mount Vernon, were carted away, leaving Beacon alone. The State House's gold dome gleams brightly on the hill today.

As you walk around, if your kids aren't history buffs, have them look for the distinctive purple panes of glass. They result from a manufacturing defect in the 19th century, but are a beautiful flaw. Hitching posts and boot scrapers are also leftovers from an earlier era. You'll trip over the many historic sites that nestle next to modern buildings. Any time you need a break, pop into the Common or Public Garden for a breather.

Jennifer Bester

A snowy day on Beacon Hill.

Boston by Neighborhood

African Meeting House/ Museum of Afro-American History

46 Joy Street
Boston, MA 02114
(617) 725-0022
www.afroammuseum.org

This is America's oldest standing African-American church. It was built in 1806 and was an important 19th-century center for the black community of Boston. The Meeting House was sometimes called Black Faneuil Hall. It was here that the New England Anti-Slavery Society was founded in 1832. The museum is next door to the Meeting House and offers tours and exhibits.

African Meeting House/ Museum of Afro-American History

Hours: Mon.-Sat., 10 a.m. - 4 p.m., Closed Thanksgiving, Christmas, and New Year's Day.

Admission: free.

Directions: Take the Red Line to Park Street Station. Walk up to Beacon Street and turn left. Take a right on Joy Street and go up the hill.

Benjamin Franklin Statue & Site of America's First Public School

45 School Street
In front of Old City Hall
Boston, MA 02108

The eight-foot-tall statue of Ben Franklin, erected in 1856, was Boston's first public portrait statue. Supposedly, one side of Franklin's face is serious, the other jovial. See if you can spot which is which. We change our mind every time we look. Near the statue is a sidewalk mosaic called the "City Carpet" marking where the first public school opened (Boston Latin). Look for Ben's name, as well as those of other famous people, such as John Hancock, spelled out in glass and ceramic pieces.

Benjamin Franklin Statue & Site of America's First Public School

Directions: Take the Orange or Blue Line to State Street.

Freedom Trail Site #6

Beacon Hill

Boston Common

Bordered by Tremont, Park, Boylston, and Beacon Streets.
Visitor's Information Center
147 Tremont Street
Boston, MA 02114
(617) 426-3115

Boston Common

Directions: Take any train to Park Street.

Freedom Trail Site #1

You won't see any cows on this former pasture, but you will see plenty of people roaming around the 40-acre-plus green space. The country's oldest park, established in 1634, was used for grazing livestock, then for hanging criminals, and now happily is just a great place to escape to from the city sidewalks. The Frog Pond (wading pool/ice-skating rink; see below for times) is located here, a big draw for young and old alike. A playground in the middle of the grounds is great for kids, but so is just running around the landscaped paths.

In the summer, the Commonwealth Shakespeare Company gives free performances at the Parkman Bandstand, which makes for a nice introduction to the Bard for youngsters. Bring a picnic and blanket.

Boston by Neighborhood

Boston Community Boating

21 Embankment Road on the Charles River
Boston, MA 02114
(617) 523-1038
www.community-boating.org

Boston Community Boating

Junior Program season (ages 10-17): mid-June to mid-August, weekdays 9 a.m. - 3 p.m.

Hours: April-October, weekdays, 1 p.m. - sunset; weekends, 9 a.m. - sunset.

Cost: $1 (!) for the Junior Program; $100 for an adult 2-day pass. For residents, $175 for the season for adults, and $135 for youths 17-22.

Directions: Take the Red Line to the Charles/MGH station. Exit the station and take a left. Go over the footbridge, cross the street, and cross another footbridge. Take the left-hand stairs.

This is one of the best deals in the city for children who live here, but you can also enjoy the boats as a visitor. If your older kids dream of learning to sail, this is a great place to start. A swimming certificate proving the ability to swim 75 yards is mandatory, as well as parental permission. New sailors start with five days of presentations, on-the-water instruction, demonstrations, and sailing with other juniors. Children can progress to skipper status and then sail by themselves. Field trips to outlying islands or the inner harbor and other activities make this an outstanding program for children. It would be wonderful even if it cost more than a buck. Adult memberships sustain the Boathouse, allowing the Junior's Program to remain such a bargain. If you are already a sailing family, take advantage of the two-day visitor's pass, available for $100 for adults (children can come as their parents' guests).

What's this "Emerald Necklace" I've heard about? It's nothing you can wear! This is a collection of parks designed by Frederick Law Olmsted (he also designed New York's Central Park). The jewels, which are all described elsewhere in this book, include Boston Common, the Public Garden, Commonwealth Mall, the Back Bay Fens, the Riverway, Olmsted Park, Jamaica Pond, Arnold Arboretum, and Franklin Park. Go to **www.emeraldnecklace.org** for more info.

Beacon Hill

Boston Massacre Site

Devonshire and State Street
Boston, MA 02109

Boston Massacre Site

Directions: Take the Orange or Blue Line to State Street. Follow the signs. The station is under the Old State House.

Freedom Trail Site #10

In front of the Old State House look for a ring of cobblestones marking the spot where five colonists were killed by British soldiers during a fight that got out of hand in March 1770. This incident was the first time blood was shed in the American Revolution.

Charles River Basin and Esplanade

Storrow Drive, Boston side of the Charles River
Boston, MA 02108

Charles River Basin and Esplanade

Directions: Take the Green Line to Arlington Street.

The Charles River Esplanade makes a wonderful setting to walk, jog, run, in-line skate, or just sit and watch the river roll on by. There are playgrounds dotted here and there on both sides of the river for kids. (Guess what? One of America's first playgrounds was on the banks of the Charles River.) Sailing can be done at Community Boating. Shows go on all summer long at the Hatch Shell. A pool complex at one end, complete with wading pool, tennis courts, and fields, offers all sorts of things to do. People line the Boston and Cambridge sides of the Charles River to watch the Head of the Charles Regatta, the Dragon Boat races, and many other annual events.

Boston by Neighborhood

Hatch Memorial Shell

Charles River, Lower Basin, Storrow Drive
Boston, MA 02114
(617) 727-9547, ext. 450

Hatch Memorial Shell

Directions: Take the Green Line to Arlington Street.

   Warm weather brings concerts and events to the half-shell shaped concert hall on the banks of the Charles River. The giant Art Deco clamshell was erected in 1940; concerts have been held on the same spot since 1910. You may have seen the Boston Pops perform the famed Fourth of July show here on TV or even braved the crowds to see it live yourself. It's an impressive sight, the fireworks bursting over the Charles River while the Pops provide background music. Free movies on Friday nights during the summer are a special treat for the whole family. We've seen the *Wizard of Oz* here, which definitely beats a drive-in in my book. Other events occur throughout the year, including free rock concerts sponsored by radio stations and classical fare as well. Get here early with a blanket to claim a spot for popular events.

King's Chapel & Burying Ground

Corner of School and Tremont Streets
Boston, MA 02114
(617) 227-2125

King's Chapel & Burying Ground

Hours: daily, 10 a.m. - 4 p.m.; closed Mondays.

Admission: free for children; adults requested to make a donation.

Directions: Take the Orange or Blue Line to State Street.

Freedom Trail Site #5

   No colonists would sell land to the Royal Governor to build a Church of England church in 1688, so he ordered one be built on the already existing burying ground. The church was too small for the congregation by 1749, so a new one was designed by Peter Harrison, America's first architect, in 1754. This was your last stop if you were to be hanged in Boston Common. The burying ground is the oldest in the city of Boston.

Beacon Hill

Massachusetts State House

Beacon Street
Boston, MA 02114
(617) 727-3676

What's old is 'new' in Boston. You'll easily find your way to the gold-domed topped "new" State House, designed by Charles Bulfinch, and built in 1798. It's the oldest building on Beacon Hill and houses the state government. Visitors on the 45-minute tour can see the Hall of Flags and the Senate and House Chambers. (The "old" State House was built in 1713.) Look for the "Sacred Cod" hanging in the House Gallery, representing the importance of the fishing industry to the city.

Massachusetts State House

Hours: Open for free tours Mon.- Fri., 10 a.m. - 3:30 p.m.

Directions: Take any train to the Park Street Station. Walk up Park Street.

Freedom Trail Site # 2

Kim Foley MacKinnon

Massachusetts State House on Beacon Hill.

Boston by Neighborhood

Museum of Science/Omni Theater/Planetarium/Computer Museum

Science Park
Boston, MA 02114
(617) 723-2500
www.mos.org

The Children's Museum is always the obvious choice to take the kids, and although there is plenty for children to do, it can be a little tedious for adults. I far prefer taking my three-year-old daughter to the Museum of Science, where there are exhibits and activities that we both can enjoy. On a recent visit, we first went to the children's section called the "Discovery Room." Exhibits range from dinosaur bone replicas that the kids can play with to a large aquarium filled with guinea pigs. When we arrived, a puppet show was just getting under way. Who knew sloths could be so funny? There's also an arts activity center, water table to splash in, climbing structure, and more. In one section of the Discovery Room, there is an infant-only area.

Out in the museum proper, one of our old favorites is a space shuttle you can climb into and pretend to blast off. A fun exhibit on the physics of playgrounds explains why you go up while your friend goes down on the teeter totter. The Computer Museum and the Museum of Science combined in 1999. One of the Computer Museum's first exhibits was an interactive digital exhibit of the ocean, called the Virtual FishTank, which allows you to program your own fish (scared, fast, colorful, hungry, etc.), release it into the water, and watch as it swims around. This was a big hit with my computer-savvy preschooler. Many grownups were spotted as well, cheering their

Fun with physics in the Discovery Center.

Beacon Hill

fish on! You can access this exhibit at home too at **www.virtualfishtank.com**. The Museum of Science can easily provide an entire day's worth of fun and is a great place to go when it's rainy. The cafeteria offers better-than-average food, and there is a huge gift shop with unique souvenirs. Visitors and locals both enjoy this museum.

For that virtual feeling you can only get with IMAX, visit the Mugar Omni Theater. This is the largest movie screen in Boston, at five stories high. Sit in the eye of a tornado or climb Mt. Everest. Also at the Museum of Science is the Charles Hayden Planetarium, where you can see an amazingly realistic night sky or take in one of their special programs that changes every six months.

> **Museum of Science/Omni Theater/Planetarium/Computer Museum**
>
> Hours: Daily, 9 a.m. - 5 p.m., Friday until 9 p.m.; summer schedule: Daily, 9 a.m. -7 p.m.; Closed Thanksgiving and Christmas.
>
> Admission: $11, adults; $8, children 3-11, seniors over 65; under 3 free. Mugar Omni Theater, Planetarium and Laser Shows are extra.
>
> Directions: Take the Lechmere Green Line to the Science Park stop. The Museum is 200 yards from the station.

New England Holocaust Memorial

Located on Congress Street near Faneuil Hall
Friends of the New England Holocaust Memorial
126 High Street
Boston, MA 02110
(617) 457-0755
www.nehm.org

> **New England Holocaust Memorial**
>
> Directions: Take the Blue or Orange Line to State Street.

Six 54-foot-tall glass towers, etched with six million numbers, makes a sobering memorial to the Holocaust's victims. The six towers are meant to represent the six main Nazi death camps, the six million Jews who died, and a menorah, all at once. Smoke rises from embers of six dark chambers named for the main death camps. The towers are lit from within at night. They are an excellent opportunity for parents to discuss an ugly chapter of history with their children, who will no doubt spot the towers if you are near downtown and Faneuil Hall.

Boston by Neighborhood

Old Corner Bookstore

Corner of School and Washington Streets
Boston, MA 02109
(617) 367-4004
www.historicboston.org

Old Corner Bookstore

Hours: Mon.-Fri., 9 a.m. - 6 p.m.;
Sat., 9 a.m. - 5 p.m.; Sunday,
noon - 5 p.m.

Directions: Take the Orange or Blue
Line to State Street.

Freedom Trail Site #7

This one-time home and apothecary shop, built in 1712, gave way to a publishing house in 1832. The *Scarlet Letter*, *Walden*, and the magazine *Atlantic Monthly* were all published here. Charles Dickens and Ralph Waldo Emerson were frequent visitors. The famous site was almost demolished to make way for a parking lot, but concerned citizens stepped in and saved the day, as often happens when a piece of local history is under threat in Boston. Today, the *Boston Globe* is the latest tenant and sells books about Boston and New England.

Old South Meeting House

310 Washington Street
Boston, MA 02109
(617) 482-6439

Old South Meeting House

Hours: daily, 9:30 a.m. - 5 p.m.

Admission: adults, $3; children 18 and under, $1.

Directions: Take the Orange or Blue Line to State Street.

Freedom Trail Site #8

This is where it all began. At least, this is where the famous Boston Tea Party began. In 1773, 5,000 colonials, angry over taxes and the Boston Massacre cheered while scores of colonists dressed in Indian garb raced out of the meeting hall, down to the harbor and dumped three shiploads of tea into the harbor. Of course, it took a couple more years and many more acts of defiance before the British tried to bring these upstarts in line. They didn't succeed. The Meeting House was built in 1729 and was the largest building in Boston at the time. Come by for a re-enactment of the famous debates.

Beacon Hill

Old State House

Corner of State and Washington Streets
Boston, MA 02109
(617) 720-3290
www.bostonhistory.org

Old State House

Hours: daily, 9 a.m. - 5 p.m.; closed New Year's Day, Thanksgiving, and Christmas.

Admission: adults, $3; children 6-18, $1.

Directions: Take the Orange or Blue Line to State Street. Follow the signs. The station is under the Old State House.

Freedom Trail Site #9

The 1713 building was at first home to the British government; later it was the first place the Declaration of Independence was heard in Massachusetts. Every July 4th, the Declaration is read from the same balcony. The Old State House is Boston's oldest public building. The lion and the unicorn sculptures are leftovers from the British Crown. Look for the cobblestone circle outside the building marking the Boston Massacre site.

At one time there was a plan to move the Old State House to the Chicago's World Fair. Of course, no self-respecting Bostonian was going to allow that to happen. In 1879, the Antiquarian Club was formed to stop the move. The club evolved into the Bostonian Society and later opened a museum of Boston's history. They also operate a library, heavy on 18th and 19th century artifacts and papers, open to museum visitors, across the street.

Boston by Neighborhood

Park Street Church & Granary Burying Ground

Park and Tremont Streets
Boston, MA 02108
(617) 523-3383
www.parkstreet.org

Park Street Church &
Granary Burying Ground

Hours: July-August, daily 9:30 a.m. - 3:30 p.m.; in winter, by appointment.

Services open to the public Sundays at 9 a.m., 10:45 a.m. and 5:30 p.m.

Take any train to the Park Street Station.

Freedom Trail Sites #3 & #4

This church, founded in 1809, is still vibrant and well-attended. Its 217-foot steeple was long the first landmark seen by travelers to the city. Abolitionists delivered many anti-slavery speeches here in the 1800s. The kids might be interested to find out that "My Country 'Tis of Thee" was first sung by the church's children's choir.

The Granary Burying Ground, next to the church, holds the remains of Samuel Adams, Paul Revere, and John Hancock, among many other famous revolutionaries. "Mother Goose," really Elizabeth Vergoose, is also buried here. It's open daily from 9 a.m. - 5 p.m. (In winter, it closes at 3 p.m.).

Best Local Playground— Boston Common Playground

Jennifer Bester

The Boston Common Playground offers a respite from sightseeing.

Right in the heart of the Common is a much-needed respite from all your traipsing about. After climbing up and down Beacon Hill or shopping at Downtown Crossing, head here to rest your weary feet. The scenery and people watching can't be beat. Grab a lemonade or fried dough from one of the many vendors while the children climb.

Back Bay

Back Bay

It really was a bay once, part of the Charles River. Actually, it was more of a swamp than a bay and was considered a health hazard. In the 1800s, it was filled in and developed over a period of 30 years. It's something to think about when you are walking around the area, where the only hazards now are to your credit cards. Today, you'll find Newbury Street fun for window-shopping, Copley Square a mecca for workers on their lunch

Boston by Neighborhood

break, and tourists gazing up at the tall towers and beautiful architecture. Commonwealth Avenue Mall is a long green walkway filled with statues and on either side, beautiful townhouses still are home to Boston's wealthiest citizens. The Public Garden is the area's contemplative spot, while the Esplanade hosts the louder events, like the Pops concert on the Fourth of July.

Boston Public Central Library

666 Boylston Street
Boston, MA 02117
(617) 536-5400
www.bpl.org

It's hard to know where to begin with the main Boston Public Library, so we'll start with all the firsts. The library, which was founded in 1848 and opened in 1854, was the first free library open to the public in the United States. It was also the first to allow patrons to borrow materials; the first to institute a branch system; and the first to set aside a separate room for children. In addition to its more than six million books, it's stocked with sculptures, murals, and paintings by famous artists, making a tour of the building a pleasure. Children love the funky wrought-iron lanterns outside, and the two giant marble lions that greet visitors on the main staircase.

Really, entering the library from the main entrance hall may make you think you are entering a museum with all the works of art. Free tours are given October through May, Sundays at 2 p.m.; Mondays at 2:30 p.m.; Tuesdays and Thursdays at 6 p.m.; and Fridays and Saturdays at 11 a.m. Don't dismiss this out of hand unless you have really antsy kids. Children are usually fascinated by all the beautiful frescoes and sculptures. If you need a breath of fresh air, visit the lovely inner courtyard in the attached McKim building.

The amount of activities at the library—free activities—is another facet that makes the library a treasure. On Friday mornings at 10:15 a.m., there is Kids' Cinema. Movies such as "Curious George Rings the Bell" or "The Little Red Hen" entertain preschoolers. Puppet shows and other special activities

The impressive Boston Public Library.

Back Bay

are scheduled throughout the year. One final note for locals, if you don't already know: the library has free or discounted passes for many museums in town. All you need is a library card. Each Boston library has different passes. Call around in advance to see if you can get what you want. I pick up a schedule each month to see what's happening at the main library. Once, my daughter got a free dance lesson from a noted local performer. All we had to do was sign up!

Colonnade Hotel Rooftop Pool

120 Huntington Avenue
Boston, MA 02116
(800) 962-3030; (617) 424-7000
www.colonnadehotel.com

Colonnade Hotel Rooftop Pool

Hours: Memorial Day-Labor Day, 9 a.m. - 6 p.m.

Admission: $20 for the day: $10 after 3 p.m.

Directions: Take the Green Line to the Hynes/ICA stop. Follow signs to Huntington Avenue.

This is one of those things that wouldn't normally occur to a parent: bringing your child to a fancy hotel for the day to hang out. But this is one of Boston's summertime treats. The rooftop pool has an excellent view of the city and is a bargain at the price when the backyard plastic wading pool won't do. A snack bar has a limited menu. Towels are provided. There are even showers and a changing area. Parents will have to serve as lifeguards.

Copley Square

Boylston Street
Boston, MA

Copley Square

Directions: Take the Green Line to Copley Square.

Copley Square, a wonderful public space surrounded by the Boston Public Library, Trinity Church, the John Hancock Building, and Boylston Street, is always a busy hub of activity. Take a minute to relax in the plaza while the children visit the Tortoise and Hare statues or chase after pigeons. The large fountain offers a soothing counterpoint to the bustle of the city around you. In the summer, there's a farmer's market where you can buy fresh fruits and vegetables. Check out the BosTix kiosk and see what half-price tickets are available for

Boston by Neighborhood

that night. Any number of restaurants and fast food joints line Boylston Street. One street over is well-heeled Newbury Street where you can window shop. It's not all adult stores either. Look for a Hello Kitty store and Niketown.

FAO Schwartz

440 Boylston Street
Boston, MA 02116
(617) 262-5900
www.fao.com

Commonwealth Avenue Mall: This mall is not a shopping center. The Mall, a swath of green in the middle of Commonwealth Avenue, runs from Boston Garden to Kenmore Square. It is part of Boston's "Emerald Necklace," the series of public parks designed by Frederick Law Olmsted.

FAO Schwartz

Directions: Take the Green Line to Copley Square.

Rob MacKinnon

You can't miss this bear at FAO Schwartz.

I may be asking for it by including a toy store here, but there's no way around it. As soon as your kids catch sight of the giant, bronze teddy bear and blocks sculpture on the sidewalk, you're done for anyway. The 12-foot-tall, 6,000-pound bear is an irresistible child-magnet. Two stories of toys, packed with everything from Barbie to bongos, will be a surefire crowd-pleaser for the kids. You can always save this place as a bribe in exchange for exploring a nearby museum or church.

Back Bay

Frog Pond

Boston Common
Boston, MA 02108
(617) 635-2120

Frog Pond

Summer: free wading pool.

Winter: ice-skating:

Hours: daily, 10 a.m. - 9 p.m.; open until 10 p.m. weekends.

Admission: adults, $3; children under 13, free. Ice-skate rentals: $5. Locker rental is $1.

Directions: Take the Red or Green Line to Park Street.

The Frog Pond has two delightful incarnations. In the summer, it serves as a gigantic wading pool with a fountain in the middle, and in winter, it's the premier place to ice-skate in Boston. Kids from all over joyfully march around the Frog Pond in their bathing suits or shorts, often joined by their hot parents or teachers as soon as the temperatures go up. In November, whether it is freezing or not, the Frog Pond is turned into an ice rink, with a little help from generators. Office workers often lace up on their lunch break, and just watching the skaters is always entertaining. Frog Pond Cottage sells snacks and hot chocolate, or you can go in just to warm up.

Institute of Contemporary Art

955 Boylston Street
Boston, MA 02115
(617) 266-5152
www.icaboston.org

Institute of Contemporary Art

Hours: Wed. & Fri., noon - 5 p.m.; Thurs., noon - 9 p.m.; weekends, 11 a.m. - 5 p.m.

Admission: $6, adults; under 12, free. Free Thursdays after 5 p.m.

Directions: Take the Green Line (B, C, or D) to the Hynes Convention Center/ICA stop.

The Institute of Contemporary Art has an ever-changing series of exhibitions, which means you'll see something new every time you visit. For now, the museum is on Boylston Street, but it is scheduled to open in larger quarters on the waterfront at Fan Pier in 2004. The whole waterfront area is under construction, like half of Boston it seems, but should be fabulous when finished. Whenever we visit, photography exhibits always draw my daughter in.

An interesting program they have, Vita Brevis, might add points of interest as you explore Boston. The program sponsors an artist to create a temporary work of art in the city. One example was an exhibit of Icelandic lava at the Fan Pier in Boston Harbor that was installed from August through September of 2001. Check out their website to see what's up when you are visiting.

Boston by Neighborhood

John Hancock Tower

200 Clarendon Street
Boston, MA 02116

John Hancock Tower

Directions: Take the Green Line to Copley Square.

Sadly, the 60th floor observatory is no longer open to the public. The terrorist events of September 11, 2001, made safety a higher priority, necessitating its closing. Although the view from the top may be missed, the I.M. Pei-designed building itself is better admired from afar. Seen from different points in the city, an optical illusion makes it look thin as a sheet of paper. It's a good way to keep your bearings getting around town. When it was near completion in the early 70s, a miscalculation of the stress of wind on the 60-story building made Bostonians run for cover as windows fell out. Don't worry. They've all been replaced, and their supports re-designed! For a great view of the Hancock, go to the Skywalk at the Prudential.

The John Hancock Building towers over sailboats in the Charles River.

Back Bay

Make Way for Ducklings Statues

Boston Public Garden (near Charles Street)
Boston, MA

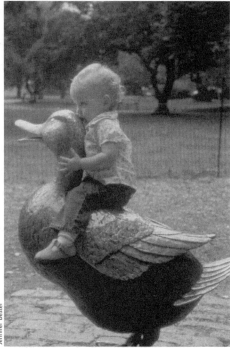

Jennifer Bester

The Make Way for Ducklings Statues always have plenty of fans in the Public Garden.

Make Way for Ducklings Statues
Directions: Take the Red Line to Park Street.

If you live in Boston, you've probably read the book to your kids at least a few dozen times. If you're not from around here or somehow just never picked up the classic *Make Way for Ducklings*, by Robert McClosky, you should. And then bring the children to the bronze sculptures of Mrs. Mallard and her brood marching along. They're big enough for the children to climb on, which usually proves an irresistible photo op for all shutterbugs. A charming event is the Duckling Parade on Mother's Day, when children dress up as ducks and march through the streets.

Boston by Neighborhood

Mapparium & Fountain at the Christian Science Center

Christian Science Center
175 Huntington Avenue
Boston, MA 02215
(617) 450-3790

Mapparium & Fountain at the Christian Science Center

Hours: Tues.-Fri., 10 a.m. - 4 p.m.; closed major holidays. Fountain on in the summer.

Admission: free.

Directions: Take the Green Line to Hynes Auditorium. Take a left on Massachusetts Ave and go three blocks.

The Christian Science Publication Society Building sounds daunting, but the huge complex on Mass. Ave. has a lot to offer children. Actually, a new research library, the Mary Baker Eddy Library for the Betterment of Humanity (another mouthful) is under construction and is scheduled to open in the fall of 2002, so call before you go. Eddy was the founder of Christian Science and the *Christian Science Monitor* newspaper.

What interests the children is the enormous fountain outside (670 x 100 feet) and the Mapparium, a gigantic stained glass globe that you can walk through. It's 30 feet in diameter and quite beautiful. It's a look at world geography as it was in 1935; updating it would be a daunting task. It doesn't matter though, walking through is pretty neat. You can whisper to each other across the room and it will sound like you are standing next to each other because of the acoustics.

Summertime, besides drawing in kids to splash in the fountain, brings all sorts of activities outside. What they call "Summer Soulstice" is a series of free events on Tuesdays at either 11 a.m. or noon. There may be participatory drumming and balloon sculpture one week, and a presentation by the Huntington Theatre Company the next. The programs are about an hour-and-a-half long, and the variety is wonderful. They even have a rain site, inside the Sunday school building.

The new library, when finished, will have some interactive exhibits to interest older children. On the way to visit the Mapparium, you'll go through the Hall of Ideas, detailing great ideas throughout history. Another exhibit will focus on the *Christian Science Monitor* and how it produces its news.

Back Bay

Public Garden

Charles Street, across from Boston Common.
(617) 635-7383

Public Garden

Directions: Take the Green Line to Arlington Street.

The Public Garden, home to the Swan Boats and the duckling statues, is a lot more than a delightful play spot for children. It was established in 1837 and is the oldest public botanical garden in the country. Hundreds of species of trees and flowers abound in the beautiful park. It's a luxurious 24 acres, right in the heart of the city. Activity is pretty low-key. Take a walk over the world's smallest suspension bridge. No biking or skating is permitted, or laying on much of the grassy areas. Children love to feed the many ducks in the lagoon and watch the Swan Boats peddle by, but for more to do, head to the Common.

Skywalk at the Prudential Tower

800 Boylston Street, 50th floor
Boston, MA 02116
(617) 859-0648

Skywalk at the Prudential Tower

Hours: daily 10 a.m. - 10 p.m.

Admission: adults, $6, under 10, $4.

Directions: Take the Green Line to the Prudential Stop.

You can take a break from shopping, as if you could actually do any with your kids anyway, and head up to the 50th floor in the Prudential Tower for a 360-degree view of Boston. It's great on a clear day, and now that the Hancock Tower is closed, this is the best view of the city, in the city. Children do like to see the world reduced in scale and are often content to just gaze out in wonder at how high they are. There are a few interactive displays around, but if you are looking for more than a bird's-eye view, save your money for something else.

Boston by Neighborhood

Swan Boats

Public Garden Lagoon
Boston, MA 02108
(617) 522-1966

This is one thing that everybody should do at least once for the sheer enjoyment value. Floating though the lagoon for 15 minutes in a giant swan peddled by foot has to be one of life's little pleasures. Oh, and the kids love it too. The Swan Boats have been in service for over a hundred years, operated by the Paget family, and are one more thing that makes Boston such a special place. Where else can you ride a swan in the middle of the city? Remember to bring along some bread to feed the ducks that follow you around. They expect it as their due.

Swan Boats at the Public Garden.

Swan Boats

Open mid-April through mid-September, weather permitting, daily..

Hours: 10 a.m. - 4 p.m.

Admission: adults, $2; children 2-15, $1.

Directions: Take the Red or Green Line to Arlington Street Station.

Tortoise & Hare Statues

Copley Square
Boylston Street
Boston, MA 02116

Tortoise & Hare Statues

Directions: Take the Green Line to Copley Square.

Keep an eye out for these two. They are near the finish line of the Boston Marathon and serve as a tribute to all who run, no matter how they place in the race. Kids love to climb on them. Let them play while you relax on benches by the fountain. Don't think you'll get anywhere near them during the actual Marathon though. Copley Square is packed with spectators for the annual event in April.

The Tortoise wins in this race on Copley Square.

Back Bay

Trinity Church

Copley Square
Boston, MA 02116
(617) 536-0944

Trinity Church
Hours: daily, 8 a.m. - 6 p.m.
Admission: free.
Directions: Take the Green Line to Copley Square stop.

With kids in tow, you probably wouldn't make this a destination alone, but it's easy to pop in if you are in the area seeing other sights. Take a break from walking around Copley Square or shopping and look into the national architectural landmark. The Romanesque-style church was built in 1877 with an active congregation. Stop by on Fridays in the school year at noon to hear free organ recitals.

Trinity Church anchors one side of Copley Square.

Best Local Playground— Clarendon Street Playground

At the corner of Clarendon Street and Commonwealth Avenue.

Take a break from Newbury Street at Back Bay's Clarendon Street Playground.

This is a top-notch playground, maintained faithfully by a neighborhood committee. Toys for all to use are a friendly touch. It's just a block from busy Newbury Street. If you tire of the playground, a walk on Commonwealth Mall is soothing. You should know that many local preschools and schools use the playground, so it can get crowded.

Boston by Neighborhood

- Haymarket
- CHRISTOPHER COLUMBUS PARK
- Boston Harbor Cruises
- Faneuil Hall
- Quincy Market
- Liberty Fleet of Tall Ships
- Custom House Tower
- Boston Light
- Dreams of Freedom Museum
- New England Aquarium & Simon's 3D IMAX Theater
- Downtown Crossing
- Friends of the New England Holocaust Memorial
- Boston Tea Party Ship & Museum
- Children's Museum
- Boston Fire Museum

Downtown & Waterfront

North
West · East
South

BOSTON COMMON

CHINATOWN

93

Downtown and the Waterfront

For convenience's sake, I am lumping these areas together, although they really cover a lot of ground. With the kids, you'll be focusing on specific sites, many of which are clustered together. You'll find more than government offices in Government Center. City Hall Plaza is packed with festivals and events in the summer. The kids will love Faneuil Hall, with all its shopping and hoopla. Long Wharf has always been the center of the harbor, and it's where you'll find tons of sightseeing boats ready to take you out to the water. The New England Aquarium and the Boston Tea Party Ship and Museum bring people flocking to the area.

Downtown & Waterfront

Boston Harbor Cruises

One Long Wharf
Boston, MA 02110
877-733-9425; (617) 227-4321
www.bostonharborcruises.com

Boston Harbor Cruises

The ticket office is located on the wharf and the cruises leave from here.

Directions: Take the T to State Street Station (via the Orange or Blue line) and follow signs to Long Wharf.

Boston Harbor Cruises, or BHC, offers a bunch of options for spending time on the water. You can take their high-speed catamaran to watch whales, visit the Boston Harbor Islands, tour the harbor itself, zip over to Provincetown on a fast ferry, or be entertained on a musical cruise. Here's a dirty, little secret that no one tells you though: many people get seasick, even on a calm sea! If you think you or your children might be one of them, take care. There is medicine you can take to combat seasickness, but it must be taken well in advance (usually four hours) of getting on the water. That said, here is a rundown on BHC's offerings.

High-Speed Catamaran Whale Watches

If you are crazy about whales, you will definitely want to do this. If you get seasick or your kids get easily bored, this is not for you. The three-hour roundtrip consists mostly of getting out to Stellwagen Bank—home of humpback, minke, and finback whales—and back. BHC promises that if you don't see a whale, they'll

High-Speed Catamaran Whale Watches

Summer schedule: departs Long Wharf 10:30 a.m. & 12:30 p.m. daily; 8:30 a.m. & 2:30 p.m. weekends; sunset cruise, 5:30 p.m. on weekends. Call for spring, fall, and holiday cruises.

Admission: adults, $29; seniors, $25; children, $23.

Three hours

give you a free ticket to try again, but that rarely happens. On a perfect September day, our family and some friends got to see "Glowstick," a young

female whale, strut her stuff. She flipped, splashed, and smacked the water with her tail to the delight of everyone onboard. A naturalist from the Whale Center of New England narrates during each whale watch, which is how we learned Glowstick's name. Bring something for the kids to do when they are tired of looking out of the windows. It's a good idea to bring a picnic along too, although there is a snack bar onboard.

Kim Foley MacKinnon

Glowstick the whale makes an appearance on a whale watch.

Boston by Neighborhood

Provincetown Fast Ferry

Just going for the 90-minute ride in this high-speed catamaran is enough of an adventure for lots of people, never mind Provincetown. Perks include a concierge who can book bike rentals for you and free admission to the Whydah Museum (filled with pirate artifacts) in Provincetown where you dock. The ferry is a little pricey, but it's a great way to avoid the hassles of driving to P-Town and makes for a fun day trip.

Provincetown Fast Ferry

The ferry runs June-October. It departs Long Wharf at 9 a.m. and returns at 4 p.m., Mon.-Thurs. On Fri.-Sun., additional runs from Boston are at 2 p.m. and 6:30 p.m. Additional returns from Provincetown are at 4 p.m. and 8:30 p.m.

Admission: adults, $25, under 12, $19, Mon.-Thurs.; fares are $45 for adults and $34 for children Fri.-Sun.

90 minutes

Harbor Islands State Park

This is a great all-day activity if the weather is nice and you need a break from the hustle and bustle of the city. In less than an hour, and a fun and informative hour at that (park rangers narrate on the way over), you are transported to one of Boston's best offerings. This state park has got it all: spectacular views, history, peace and quiet. An added bonus is that there are no cars here; you don't need to worry about little ones getting run over (believe me, this is

Jennifer Bester

A quiet walk on George's Island in Boston Harbor.

a wonderful thing after facing Boston drivers!). Pack a picnic, sunscreen, and a Frisbee, and you'll have a memory in the making. If you just have a day, I'd stick with one island, although you can visit others on a free water taxi. Camping is available on certain islands. Advance reservations required.

George's Island, with 28 acres, is the park's centerpiece, and where the ferry docks. There's a visitor's center, picnic grounds, snack bar, toilets, and a beach (no swimming though). Fort Warren was built here between 1833 and 1869. It is a

Harbor Islands State Park

Ferry service is available from Long Wharf (next to the New England Aquarium). Bay State Cruises ((617) 723-7800) transports passengers to Georges Island, where you can catch a free water taxi to the other islands.

Directions: Take the Red Line to South Station. It's then a 10-minute walk down Atlantic Avenue, right past the Boston Harbor Hotel.

Ferry service is every hour, on the hour, from 10 a.m. - 5 p.m., weather permitting. Call to make sure it's running if the weather seems iffy to you.

Cost: $8 for adults; $6 for children 12 and under.

45 minutes by ferry from downtown.

Downtown & Waterfront

National Historic Landmark and was used as a prison for Confederate soldiers during the Civil War. Exploring the fort is an adventure in itself. Tours are sometimes offered by park rangers. Call for times.

My family and a few friends with children went to George's Island in the summer, and everyone loved it. The ferry alone is a big treat for younger children. Don't be afraid of lugging a big cooler (with plenty of water). A nice touch on the island is that at the dock you'll find free wooden wheelbarrows available to haul your stuff (or your kids) around. A word of warning, except for inside the fort, there is not a lot of shade here, so an umbrella is a good idea to give you a break from the sun.

Boston Fire Museum

344 Congress Street
Boston, MA 02210
(617) 482-1344

Boston Fire Museum

Hours: summerttime only, Saturdays, noon - 4 p.m.

Admission: free.

Directions: Take the Red Line to South Station. Walk up Atlantic Avenue to Congress.

The little 1899 firehouse makes for a charming visit if you can time it right—and if your children are fire engine fanatics. Open only in the summer for a few hours on Saturdays means you have to plan in advance, although if you can get someone to call you back, you might be able to schedule a better time to visit. Inside the museum, there are antique fire equipment and photos. Children can play with and climb on some of the equipment.

Boston by Neighborhood

Boston Light

Little Brewster Island

Boston Harbor, Boston, MA 02110
(617) 223-8666
www.bostonislands.com

Little Brewster Island

Open Memorial Day-Labor Day, Fri-Sun.

Admission: Saturday & Sunday adults $25; children 6-12, $15; under 5, free. (On Fridays, adults, $29.)

Directions: Leave from JFK Library, Columbia Point, or Fan Pier, Boston. Call for times.

Well, this little adventure will set you back some cash, but if lighthouses are your kid's thing, this is where you want to go. Boston Light is, you guessed it, America's oldest light station. Your admission gets you a three-and-a-half hour ranger-guided tour. This includes an hour narration on the boat, where you'll spot three other lighthouses on the way to Little Brewster Island. You spend an hour-and-a-half on the island itself, which is less than two acres in size, and you can meet the last official light keepers in the country. The original lighthouse was built in 1716, but the British destroyed most of it in the Revolutionary War. It was rebuilt in 1783. It stands 102 feet tall, and you can climb up to the top on your visit (up 76 stairs and two ladders). The U.S. Coast Guard, which runs the lighthouse, was all set to automate it in 1990, like every other lighthouse in the country, when preservation groups protested (we're so good at protesting here!). So, the Coast Guard mans the lighthouse. If you can swing it, this really is a fascinating tour, and you can't beat the view from the lighthouse. Here's a piece of trivia for the kids: the beacon can be seen for 27 miles.

Downtown & Waterfront

Boston Tea Party Ship & Museum

Congress Street Bridge
Boston, MA 02210
(617) 338-1773
www.bostonteapartyship.com

Try your hand at throwing tea off the ship.

Boston Tea Party Ship & Museum

Hours: spring/fall 9 a.m. - 5 p.m.; summer, 9 a.m. - 6 p.m. Closed Dec.- March.

Admission: adults, $8; children, $4; under 4, free.

Directions: Take the Red Line to South Station. Go toward the water on Atlantic Avenue, then take a left on Congress Street.

At press time, the ship was closed due to a fire in the summer of 2001, but it is slated to be repaired and re-open in 2002. Call ahead. If you're anywhere near the Museum Wharf, you'll spot the ship. *Brig Beaver II* is a re-creation of the smallest of three ships that colonists boarded in that famous December night of 1773. Dressed as Native Americans, the colonists, or "Sons of Liberty," dumped more than 300 crates of tea into the harbor as a protest against unfair taxes. You know how the story ends. Your kids might not be so familiar with our country's history, however, and this is a fun place to educate them. It has all things children like. It's outside, it's loud, and they get to throw things. Start off at the mock protest, with fully costumed patriots leading the debates, and then climb on board to dump some crates of your own (they are empty and on ropes to be pulled up later). The reenactments are scheduled every half-hour so you will be sure to catch one. You can explore the ship and its exhibits, watch a couple of films about the events, and of course, have a cup of tea.

Boston by Neighborhood

Children's Museum

300 Congress Street
Boston, MA 02210
(617) 426-8855
www.bostonkids.org

Children's Museum

Hours: daily 10 a.m. - 5 p.m.; Friday until 9 p.m.

Admission: adults, $7; children 2-15, $6; under 1, free. Friday nights are Family Dollar Night. Admission is $1 per person from 5 - 9 p.m.

Directions: Take the Red Line to South Station. Walk around the Federal Reserve Building and down to the water. The museum is behind the giant Hood Milk Bottle.

Although I always vote for the Museum of Science, many would argue with me that the Children's Museum can't be beat. I have to agree that it is lots of fun for children and you probably never see an unhappy kid there, unless it's time for him or her to leave. Three levels of interactive activities and exhibits can keep children busy all day long. Families with small children (under three) should head straight for the Smith Family Playspace on the second floor. There is even a protected infant area with appropriate toys. An outstanding feature is the Family Resource Room where moms can go nurse, and parents can catch up on all the latest parenting information in the library. You can even grab a cup of coffee here, which you might need to keep up with your kids.

Out of the toddler area there are many options for the kids to explore. My daughter likes to go up to Grandparents' Attic on the fourth floor to play dress up. Nearby is the Arthur's World exhibit, a recreation of that famous aardvark's house, school, and tents (for when he goes camping). There is also a stage on this floor, with shows taking place periodically. Tickets are free but limited, so you should pick them up when you first come into the museum. The Supermercado is also very popular, where kids can pretend they are at a Latin American supermarket. Older kids will like the rock-climbing structure (adults can climb too!). There are many other exhibits, and you probably won't be able to visit them all in one day.

If it is warm out, you can have lunch outside at the giant Hood Milk Bottle, which sells snacks (don't forget to get your hand stamped when you leave the museum so you can go back in). If you brought your own picnic, you can go to the Lunch Room on the first floor, or, (you've got to love this) there is a McDonald's adjacent to the museum.

Got milk? Outside the Children's Museum.

Downtown & Waterfront

Chinatown

Bordered by Kneeland Street, Tremont Street, Atlantic Avenue and Summer Street

Boston's Chinatown is the third largest in the country, although you'd never guess it. It is very small, but packed tight, and located right next to the Downtown Crossing shopping area (see below). Go to the Chinatown stop on the Orange Line, if you want to hop out and explore. Kids will probably enjoy the Chinatown gates, standing 36 feet tall, at the entrance to the area. Four marble Chinese dogs, weighing in at 3,000 pounds each, stand guard. They were a gift from Taiwan. Eating and shopping are the main tourist activities here. Look for the phone booths topped with colorful pagodas.

Custom House Tower

3 McKinley Square
Boston, MA 02109
(617) 310-6300

Custom House Tower

Hours: Tours daily at 10 a.m. & 4 p.m., Sat., 4 p.m. only. No tours in inclement weather.

Admission: free, but donation requested.

Directions: Take the Blue Line to the Aquarium stop.

The Custom House Tower is officially called the Marriott Custom House, which means what you think it means. It wasn't always so. The Custom House was built in 1847, and when the 30-foot tower was added in 1915, it became the city's first skyscraper. The beautiful clock tower is often photographed and a familiar sight to many. The Marriott Vacation Club International refurbished the Custom House, doing such a good job in preserving it, while also turning it into a luxury hotel, that it won a 1999 National Preservation Honor Award from the National Trust for Historic Preservation. Today, you can take a guided tour, providing the weather cooperates.

Boston by Neighborhood

Downtown Crossing

Intersection of Washington Street with Winter and Summer Streets.

Famous Filene's Basement and dozens of other stores are located in this pedestrian-only shopping area downtown. Maybe your kids like shopping (mine doesn't), but all the bustling activity outside is always entertaining. You can always take your children to the annual wedding dress sale at the Basement as a lesson on how NOT to behave.

A visit to Filene's Basement is a must in Downtown Crossing.

Downtown Crossing

Directions: Take any inbound train to the Downtown Crossing or Park Street stops.

Dreams of Freedom Museum

One Milk Street
Boston, MA 02109
(617) 338-6022
www.dreamsoffreedom.org

This museum is a great introduction to Boston's immigrant history, and its interactive displays will definitely interest older children. Popping in here for an hour (that's about all it takes to walk through) is an education in how immigrants came to Boston and how they felt. Neat features like having your "passport" stamped as you make your way though customs or meeting Boston characters who give first-hand descriptions of their arrival keeps things lively.

Dreams of Freedom Museum

Hours: January to mid-April, Tues. - Sun., 10 a.m. - 5 p.m.; mid-April to December, daily, 10 a.m. - 6 p.m.

Admission: adults, $7.50; children 6-18, $3.50.

Directions: Take any train to Park Street. From Park St., cross Tremont St. Walk down Winter St. to Washington St. and take a left. Take a right on Milk St.

Downtown & Waterfront

Faneuil Hall Marketplace & Quincy Market

4 South Market Building, Congress Street
Boston, MA 02109
(617) 523-1300
www.faneuilhallmarketplace.com

Faneuil Hall Marketplace & Quincy Market

Directions: Take the Green Line to Government Center. Cross City Hall Plaza.

Freedom Trail Site # 11

Faneuil Hall (FAN-yul) was built in 1742 as a public meeting and marketplace. Quincy Market was built next door in the 1800s, as more space was needed. Boston picked up its "Cradle of Liberty" nickname from the goings-on here because of the many important speeches about freedom that occurred in the Colonial era. Today, the area is a major tourist draw, packed with stores and restaurants. Look for the four-foot copper grasshopper weathervane on top of Faneuil Hall. (Why a grasshopper? No one knows.)

Two stories of eateries and shops entice young and old alike into Quincy Market. This is a good quick-food stop, but you'll be among lots of tourists. Artists and street performers entertain outside.

HarborWalk

The HarborWalk is a work-in-progress. Construction on the waterfront, to include a new convention center, hotels, shops, and museum is eagerly awaited by the city. For now, it runs from Long Wharf to the fish pier. Along the route you'll find the Aquarium, Rowes Wharf, the Boston Tea Party Museum and Ship, and Museum Wharf, where the Children's Museum is located. There are plenty of places to stop and eat or shop. Children will simply enjoy running back and forth, looking at all the ships and boats coming in and out of the harbor.

Boston by Neighborhood

Haymarket

Around the corner from Quincy Market.
Open Friday & Saturday

Haymarket

Directions: Take the Green or Orange Line to the Haymarket stop.

On Fridays and Saturdays you might be drawn to the loud commotion near Quincy Market. There's nothing wrong. It's just the loud vendors at Haymarket trying to entice buyers to buy fruit, fish, and vegetables at Boston's outdoor food market. This market has been here for 200 years, believe or not. If your kids want a lesson in how haggling really works, pop on by. Hold on tight to your kids—it is always packed with jostling customers, and they're not too polite if you get in their way (beware of bad language, too!). One more warning for both you and the kids: no touching allowed. What you see is what you get.

Liberty Fleet of Tall Ships

Ticket office: 67 Long Wharf
Boston, MA 02110
(617) 742-0333
www.libertyfleet.com

Liberty Fleet of Tall Ships

Hours: June-Sep.: daily two-hour sails at noon, 3 p.m., and 6 p.m. Sunday brunch sail, 11 a.m.

Admission: daily sails, $30 for adults; $18 under 12. Brunch: $45, adults; $25, under 12.

Directions: Departs from Long Wharf

There is nothing like sailing around Boston Harbor in one of these beautiful tall ships that come to visit in the summer. The *Liberty Clipper* and the *Liberty* both offer two-and-a-half hour tours where you can relax on deck or join in and help the crew with hoisting the sails. Drinks are available to buy on board, but bring your own snacks. Anyone who truly longs to be on the water won't be able to pass up the 18th century replicas of schooners.

Downtown & Waterfront

New England Aquarium & Simon's 3D IMAX Theater

Central Wharf
Boston, MA 02110
(617) 973-5200
www.neaq.org

We always find the Aquarium a soothing, mysterious place to be. We talk a little more softly in here. The darkened halls highlight the animals swimming in tanks. Our all-time favorite is the giant ocean tank that is the centerpiece of the museum. The 200,000-gallon tank, formally named the Caribbean Coral Reef Exhibit, is a 24-foot-deep reef filled with caves, reefs, sharks, turtles, and hundreds of tropical fish. A winding ramp leads up around the tank and visitors can peek in windows as they stroll up four stories to the top. Smaller children will love the tide pool exhibit where they can get wet and hold starfish. Special activities such as playing with sea lions are available (for an additional cost). The Aquarium also offers whale watches and harbor tours.

Discovering the joys of starfish at the New England Aquarium.

Boston by Neighborhood

Simon's IMAX Theater

If you worry that our 24/7 media culture has rendered the next generation jaded to visual wonder, you are in for a happy surprise when you bring them to the New England Aquarium's new giant-screen theater. The beautiful 300-seat theater occupies its own building adjacent to the Aquarium, which it dwarfs with its many stories-tall screen. But the effect of the films—which take up aquatic themes—is much more than bigger-is-better. This is as close to scuba diving as most of you are going to get.

Some of the IMAX films screened at the Aquarium are shot with 3-D technology, which has the effect of making the images on the 84-foot screen appear as if they are floating just inches in front of your face. The effect is so real that younger children often wave their hands in front of them, attempting to reach out and touch what they see. Older children and adults will also be spellbound, especially those with an interest in wildlife or an adventurous spirit. Any child who is old enough to sit still and wear glasses will enjoy the spectacle. And grown ups who can't imagine a school of ocean mackerel capable of making them gasp—think again. Highly recommended.

New England Aquarium
& Simon's 3D IMAX Theater

Hours: July 1-Labor Day, Mon., Tues., Fri., 9 a.m. - 6 p.m.; Wed.-Thurs., 9 a.m. - 8 p.m.; Sat.-Sun., 9 a.m. - 7 p.m. Labor Day-June 30, Mon.-Fri., 9 a.m. - 5 p.m.; Sat. Sun., 9 a.m. - 6 p.m.

Admission: adults, $13; children 2-11, $7; under 3, free.

Directions: Take the Orange or Blue line to the State Street/Aquarium stop.

Simon's IMAX Theater

Several morning and afternoon shows daily, additional shows Fri. and Sat. evenings.

Admission: adults, $7.50; children, $5.50.

Downtown & Waterfront

Best Local Playground— Christopher Columbus Park

This playground, with its climbable crow's nest (toddlers beware), is located right on Commercial Wharf. It's perfect for kids to pretend they are sailing off to sea. You can sit and watch the action in the harbor or wander over to Rose Kennedy's Rose Garden. There's lots of shade and a fountain to splash around in if it's hot. Joe's American Bar & Grill is next to the park if you want a bite (kid's menu available).

Christopher Columbus Park is right on the waterfront.

Boston by Neighborhood

Fenway

The Fenway, home to the Boston Red Sox and the Museum of Fine Arts, is sometimes called the Avenue of the Arts. This area really grew up in the early 1900s, when many institutions started building over here. Huntington Avenue, the main stretch, has museums and theatres vying for your attention in this cultural center. (You'll

find theatres listed in Chapter Four.) Fenway Park was built in 1912 in Kenmore Square. On game days, the area is a mob scene before and after games, and so is the "B" train on Green Line. You can't miss the famous double-sided neon CITGO billboard if you're in the area.

Back Bay Fens

The Back Bay Fens is part of Boston's Emerald Necklace. You'll find it behind the Museum of Fine Arts, along the banks of the Muddy River. Take the Green Line to the MFA stop. In a previous life it was a marsh, which was drained and filled in, and then turned into parkland. It is fun to walk through the Victory Gardens, the nation's oldest remaining WWII gardens. There is also a rose garden, absolutely stunning in bloom, and myriad pathways to explore. This is a good place to wander around if you need a break from the nearby museums and some fresh air.

Fenway

Fenway Park & Tours

4 Yawkey Way
Boston, MA 02215
(617) 236-6666
www.redsox.mlb.com

Fenway Park & Tours

Tickets: start at $18. There are special discount days when you can get a ticket for as little as $9. Call for details.

Tours: May-August, Mon.-Fri., on the hour, 9 a.m. - noon; 2 p.m. (Tour offered if no game that day). Adults are $6; under 15, $4.

Directions: Take the Green Line to the Fenway Station.

Built in 1912, Fenway Park is the last original ballpark in the American League. This is the best reason to take your kids there, but it is also the best reason to stay away. Fenway is a piece of Americana—one that won't be around for long (or not in its present form). As this book goes to press, the ballpark's future is uncertain. Red Sox diehards and historical preservationists see the park's character and uniqueness, but a lot of others see nothing but a really decrepit old stadium. Fenway lacks the amenities that make a long sporting event comfortable for adults, let alone children. Furthermore, the ballpark management doesn't seem particularly interested in making Fenway child-friendly. Newer stadiums offer play areas for kids' inevitable lapses in attention. Some parks let kids run the bases after a game. At Fenway, they serve beer on Kids' Opening Day (the first Saturday of the season). Parents have complained of excessive drinking and bad language in the bleachers, with nearby cops paying no heed. For this reason, you might want to consider grandstand seats, though they are expensive. This is more an older kid activity and then only for those really interested in baseball.

That said, what I do recommend doing here is a behind-the-scenes tour if you are around in the summer. You get to see the pressroom, the 600 Club, privates suites, and best of all, you'll get on the field. You can even touch the "Green Monster" and sit in the dugout. The tour is about an hour.

At night, look for the CITGO sign flashing in Kenmore Square. Through the years plans to take down the sign have met with such protest from Bostonians that it is sure to stay a familiar icon for decades to come.

Boston by Neighborhood

Isabella Stewart Gardner Museum

280 The Fenway
Boston, MA 02115
(617) 566-1401
www.boston.com/gardner

Isabella Stewart Gardner Museum

Hours: Tues.-Sun., 11 a.m. - 5 p.m. Closed Mondays and Thanksgiving and Christmas.

Admission: adults, $10 ($11 on weekends); under 18, free.

Directions: Take the Green Line to the Museum of Fine Arts stop.

The Gardner Museum, a wonderful place left exactly as it was when Isabella Stewart Gardner was alive, as per her wishes, can be great to explore with children. It might not seem that way at first, though. Gardner designed the museum as a Venetian palace and opened three floors to the public in 1903. She lived on the fourth floor until her death in 1924. It is a smaller museum and the rooms circle the garden courtyard, which always has blooming plants (a welcome sight in the winter).

Pick up the family guides available at the info desk on your way in. One is called "Eyes on Fenway Court." You'll explore the beautiful inner courtyard of the museum and look for various works of art with clues like this from the guide: "I am a dolphin made out of stone. I am a twin. I am not alone. Look near the fountain, that's where we'll be, with our squiggly tails, we swim in the sea! Can you find me?" You've got rhymes, a treasure hunt and culture rolled into one. Another guide, "Small Wonders," points out the tinier objects in the collection often overlooked. Your kids will love spotting objects before you do. The Gardner has a series called "Family Fun Programs" held a few times a year on Saturday mornings. It is for children ages 6 though 10 accompanied by an adult. The cost is $20 a pair, and after exploring the galleries, you go to the art studio to try your hand at whatever the focus is that day, for example, drawing or sculpting. The museum also has a café with great food.

Fenway

Museum of Fine Arts

465 Huntington Avenue
Boston, MA 02115
(617) 267-9300

Museum of Fine Arts, Boston

Exploring exhibits at the MFA.

    The Museum of Fine Arts (MFA) is huge and can be intimidating to the uninitiated, or the very small. Rather than aimlessly dragging your kids around in an effort to find something that interests them, come on the weekend and stop by the Family Place (open Sat. and Sun., Oct.-June, 10 a.m. - 4 p.m.). You can begin the visit by playing games or working on puzzles. Museum instructors help you get going with suggestions and interesting facts. Activity books (always available at the Info Center) have self-guided tours. Depending on your child, you might decide to pick up "Fabulous Beasts West to East" or "Unravel the Mystery of the Mummy." Afterschool programs for children ages 6-12 are also available on a

Boston by Neighborhood

drop-in basis Mondays through Fridays during the school year from 3:30 p.m. - 4:45 p.m. Kids will explore different galleries and do projects with museum staff. The program is free.

If you decide to head off on your own, it's a good idea to have a game plan in mind first. Pick two or three exhibits you want to visit, then call it quits. Nobody likes a cranky kid in a museum. The Egyptian Gallery is a no-brainer; kids always like the mummies. The Modern Art Gallery can make for interesting discussions. The Art of Africa Gallery fascinates children with beautiful masks.

There are three different food venues—an upscale restaurant with upscale prices, a café, and a cafeteria. Those with kids will probably want to stick to the cafeteria downstairs. Stop by the gift shop on the way out. It has a large selection of toys and books for children that you won't find anywhere else.

> **Museum of Fine Arts**
>
> Hours: daily, 10 a.m. - 4:45 p.m.; Wed.-Fri., open until 9:45 p.m. (Only the West Wing is open late Thurs. and Fri. Tickets are $2 less after 5 p.m.). Closed Thanksgiving and Christmas.
>
> Admission: $14, adults; children 7-17, $5 until 3 p.m. (after 3 p.m., free); under 7, free. Your ticket allows you to visit twice in a 30-day period. After 4 p.m. on Wednesday, admission is by voluntary contribution.
>
> Directions: Take the Green Line to the Museum of Fine Arts stop. It's across the street.

Best Local Playground

There aren't any close playgrounds in this area. Your best bet is heading toward the Back Bay Fens and strolling along. There is plenty of green space for the kids to roam around.

North End

North End

The North End is the city's Italian section, and you'll have no doubt about where you are while there. There is a real European feel to the area, and food is a huge part of the neighborhood. You'll be tripping over bakeries and restaurants as you wander around the narrow streets. Every weekend in the summer, saints are celebrated with processions and festivals, and lots of delicious, garlicky food. Since two of the Freedom Trail sites are located here (Paul Revere's House and the Old North Church), see if you can time your walk to coincide with lunch or dinnertime. Close your eyes, spin around and point. Eat there. You can't go wrong at any of the restaurants here.

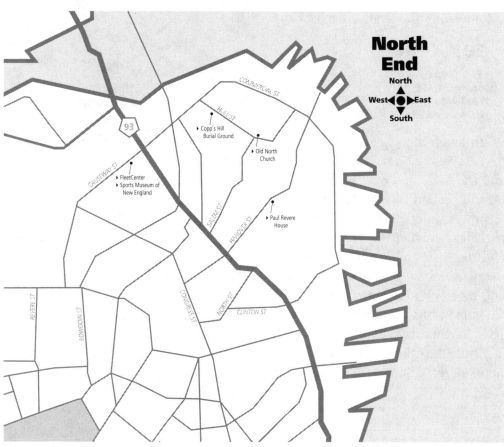

Boston by Neighborhood

Copp's Hill Burial Ground

Hull Street, uphill from the Old North Church
Boston, MA 02113

The second-oldest burial ground in Boston is Copp's Hill, formerly called Windmill Hill. William Copp was a shoemaker who owned the land at one point. Many of the North End's artisans and merchants were buried here, along with free black people who lived in what was called the "New Guinea Community." Robert Newman, the Old North Church sexton who warned Paul Revere that the British were coming, is also buried here. The British took aim from here at Charlestown during the Battle of Bunker Hill (that we all know was really Breed's Hill).

> **Copp's Hill Burial Ground**
>
> Hours: daily, 9 a.m. - 5 p.m. (in the winter until 3 p.m.)
>
> Admission: free.
>
> Directions: Take the Orange or Green Line to Haymarket Station. Walk under the expressway to Cross Street. Follow the red painted Freedom Trail line to Salem Street.
>
> Freedom Trail Site #14

FleetCenter

One FleetCenter Place
Boston, MA 02114
(617) 787-7678
www.fleetcenter.com

> **FleetCenter**
>
> Directions: Take the Orange or Green Line to North Station.

Although the FleetCenter opened in 1995, it still is considered new in these parts. That's not so unusual when you consider both the "new" State House and the "old" one were both built before 1800. Anyway, although diehard Boston Garden fans still complain about its loss, the shiny new FleetCenter has much to offer, such as comfort and visibility, two things that I like when parked somewhere for a couple of hours. The Boston Bruins (NHL ice hockey) and the Boston Celtics (NBA basketball) both call the FleetCenter home, but many other events happen here year-round. The circus, ice shows, concerts, and more are just part of the schedule. The 2001 U.S. Figure Skating Championships were held here, and the first and second rounds of the 2003 NCAA Men's Basketball Tournament are scheduled for the FleetCenter. In addition, the Sports Museum of New England is located on the fifth and sixth floors of the complex. (See pg. 61 for details on the museum.)

North End

Old North Church

193 Salem Street
Boston, MA 02113
(800) 981-4776; (617) 523-4848
www.oldnorth.com

Old North Church

Hours: June-October, daily 9 a.m. - 6 p.m.; November-May, 9 a.m. - 5 p.m.

Basic tour free, donations welcome; Behind the Scenes Tour in June-October is $8 for adults; $5 for children under 16. "Paul Revere Tonight" tickets are $12 for adults; $8, under 12. Summer shows. Call for times.

Directions: Take the Orange or Green Line to Haymarket. Walk under the expressway to Cross Street. Follow the red painted Freedom Trail line to Salem Street.

Freedom Trail Site #13

Two lanterns swinging from the belfry in the Old North Church set in motion Paul Revere's famous ride, harbinger of the Revolutionary War. The sexton of the church, Robert Newman (who is buried in Copp's Hill), hung the lanterns on April 18, 1775, to warn that the British were coming up the Charles River, en route to Lexington. The Old Church is still open for services and welcomes visitors. It was built in 1723 and is quite beautiful. In addition to its Paul Revere fame, the church is home to the oldest church bells in North America. The Old North Church's gardens are a wonderful spot to rest if you are walking the Freedom Trail. Children might enjoy the "Paul Revere Tonight" show, where a costumed actor recounts this famous citizen's early years in Boston.

Boston by Neighborhood

Paul Revere House

19 North Square
Boston, MA 02113
(617) 523-2338
www.paulreverehouse.org

Paul Revere House

Hours: Mid-April-October, 9:30 a.m. - 5:15 p.m.; November-April 14, 9:30 a.m. - 4:15 p.m.; closed Mondays January-March.

Admission: adults, $2.50; children 5-17, $1.

Directions: Take the Green or Orange Line to Haymarket Station.

Freedom Trail Site #12

Unless your kid is doing a report on Paul Revere or you are interested in early Boston architecture, this is probably a stop to skip. Paul Revere owned the house from 1770 through 1800, and this is where he departed on his famous ride. The house is the oldest remaining building in the downtown area. It was built around 1680 and much of the original building is intact. If you do go, it's a pretty quick walk-through.

I recommend scheduling a visit to coincide with one of the many events held throughout the year at the museum. On Saturdays, May through October, programs about life in colonial Boston are fascinating to children.

Everything from music to cutting silhouettes is demonstrated. Occasionally actors portray Revere and his wife, his mother-in-law and many others, and answer questions about their roles during the Revolutionary War. Going to one of these programs is probably more engaging to children than a mere tour around the museum. Check their website for current events.

Greater Boston Convention and Visitors Bureau

Paul Revere Statue & Old North Church Steeple.

North End

Sports Museum of New England

On the 5th & 6th floors of the FleetCenter
Causeway Street
Boston, MA 02114
(617) 624-1235
www.sportsmuseum.org

For the sports fans in the family, this is an essential stop. Exhibits cover the gamut—boxing, hockey, football, basketball, soccer, and baseball. Pretend you're catching a fastball from Roger Clemens at one interactive exhibit, watch old footage of the Boston Garden (true fans still lament its demise, but you can sit in old Garden seats at least!), and learn about local high school and college teams. Don't miss the Boston Bruins Hall of Fame portraits or the exhibit on the Boston Marathon.

Sports Museum of New England

Hours: schedule depends on FleetCenter events. Always call ahead. Generally open Tues.-Sat., 11 a.m. - 5 p.m. and Sun., noon - 5 p.m.

Admission: adults, $6; children 6-17, $4; under 6, free. Buy your tickets at the FleetCenter box office.

Directions: Take the Orange or Green Line to North Station.

Best Local Playground— Langone Park

Commercial Street

This sweet little playground has got one of the best views in town and everything you need for relaxing after wandering around the North End. It even has a public bathroom, a nice clean one, modeled after those in Paris. You'll have to pay a quarter to use it, but I've had to spend a lot more at various restaurants or coffee shops to gain access to the toilet. Anyway, the playground sits right on the edge (almost) of the Charles River. It's enclosed, has swings and a climbing structure, and a nearby spray fountain at the Mirabella Pool next door is great in hot weather.

Boston by Neighborhood

Charlestown

Charlestown is actually older than Boston, by one year. Ten Puritan families settled Charlestown in 1629, and it remained its own community until 1874, when it was annexed to Boston. Learn about the famous 1775 Battle of Bunker Hill (AKA Breed's Hill) at the monument. The town was pretty much destroyed by the famous battle and then rebuilt after the American Revolution. The Charlestown Navy Yard, no longer in operation, is a national historic monument and home to the USS *Constitution*. Tours of the ship and the nearby museum offer a fascinating look into its glorious past.

Charlestown

Bunker Hill Monument

Monument Square
Charlestown, MA 02129
(617) 241-7575

Bunker Hill Monument

Hours: daily, 9 a.m. - 4:30 p.m.

Admission: free.

Directions: Take the Orange or Green Line to North Station. Walk down Causeway Street to N. Washington Street. Turn left, cross the Charlestown Bridge. Follow the Freedom Trail line.

Freedom Trail Site #16

The first major battle of the Revolutionary War took place on Breed's Hill, so we have a monument on Bunker Hill. We actually lost this battle, but have a monument anyway. Breed's Hill was a better vantage point than the taller Bunker Hill for the colonists to try to repel the British. They managed to fight off two waves of attacks from the British, killing half of them, before retreating. Although losing the battle, this proved the colonists could really fight and gave them hope for future battles.

You can climb up the 221-foot-high monument for great views of the city. Little kids may not do so well on this trek. Go to the Bunker Hill Pavilion to learn more on the battle in a movie called "Whites of Their Eyes." The name of the movie comes from the legend that the colonists weren't supposed to fire until they saw the whites of the Redcoats' eyes.

Charlestown Navy Yard

National Historical Park
Charlestown, MA 02129
(617) 242-5601

Charlestown Navy Yard

Admission: free.

Directions: Take the Orange or Green Line to North Station. Walk down Causeway Street to N. Washington Street. Turn left, cross the Charlestown Bridge. Follow the Freedom Trail line. You can also catch a water shuttle from Long Wharf near the Aquarium (call Boston Harbor Cruises for details, (617) 227-4320).

The Charlestown Navy Yard, now part of the park system, was a thriving shipyard for 174 years. It was one of the first shipyards built in the United States, but before that, the British landed troops on the spot before the Battle of Bunker Hill. You can walk around and see what remains of the shipyard, but the biggest draw here is the USS *Constitution*.

Boston by Neighborhood

USS Constitution and Museum

Charlestown Navy Yard
Box 1812
Boston, MA 02129
(617) 426-1812
www.ussconstitutionnavy.mil
www.ussconstitutionmuseum.org

USS *Constitution* and Museum

Admission: both are free.

Hours: Ship—tours given Thursday-Sunday, noon - 4 p.m. Museum—open May-Nov., 9 a.m. - 6 p.m.; Dec. - Apr., 10 a.m. - 5 p.m.

Directions: See Charlestown Navy Yard above.

Freedom Trail Site #15

"Old Ironsides," as the oldest commissioned warship afloat is affectionately called, makes its home at the Charlestown Navy Yard. If you ever get a chance to see the ship out in the harbor, it's a sight you'll never forget. Crewmembers give tours of the vessel, which was built in 1797, at various intervals. The *Constitution* is most renowned for fending off five British ships in a battle that occurred during the War of 1812. Visit the nearby museum for exhibits, hands-on activities, and artifacts detailing the long history of the warship.

Best Local Playground— Paul Revere Park

The Paul Revere Park on Constitution Road in Charlestown is a fabulous place to make a stop after visiting the USS *Constitution* and Bunker Hill, especially if you climbed up the monument! There's five acres for roaming or picnicking, a fenced-in playground, and a great view. You're right on the Charles River.

Jamaica Plain/Roxbury/Dorchester

Jamaica Plain/Roxbury/Dorchester

These three neighborhoods, once home to the richest Bostonians, are part of the city, but often get a bad rap or are ignored altogether. Although their fortunes fell, they are on the rise again. There are some sights definitely worth seeking out in these areas. Jamaica Plain, or "JP" to those who live there, is the latest urban renewal success story. The area prides itself on its diversity. The main drag, Centre Street, is packed with every type of cuisine, from Thai to Latino to Indian. Jamaica Pond is a serene setting in the thriving neighborhood. The Franklin Park Zoo in Roxbury is one of those jewels in the Emerald Necklace. In Dorchester, two popular sites to visit are the JFK Library & Museum, and the city's major paper, the *Boston Globe*.

Boston by Neighborhood

Arnold Arboretum

125 Arborway
Jamaica Plain, MA 02130
(617) 524-1718
www.arboretum.harvard.edu

Arnold Arboretum

Hours: dawn to dusk daily.

Admission: free.

Directions: Take the Orange Line to Forest Hills. Take a right up South Street. Five minute walk.

Jennifer Bester

Wide paths give plenty of space for walkers at the Arnold Arboretum.

Come here and forget that you are in Boston. More than 250 acres of open space makes this easy to do. You can bike, in-line skate, run, or just stroll among the walkways in this beautiful park, yet another Boston jewel in Frederick Law Olmsted's Emerald Necklace. The only thing you can't do here is picnic, tempting as it may be. Oh, you can't pick anything or climb anything either—the Arboretum is a National Historic Landmark and part of Harvard University. This is a wonderful place for city-dwellers to bring their kids to learn how to ride their bikes or to show them there is more to the world than sidewalks and stoplights. Lilac Sunday (on Mother's Day) in May is the one exception to the no-picnicking rule and brings crowds of people to celebrate the spring and flowers.

Boston Globe

135 Morrissey Boulevard
Dorchester, MA 02107
(617) 929-2653

Boston Globe

Tours given Monday & Thursday, 10 a.m., 11:15 a.m. & 1 p.m., by appointment only, and one Wednesday night a month.

Admission: free.

Children must be over 9 years old.

Directions: Take the Red Line to the JFK/UMASS stop. Walk down Morrissey Boulevard.

For a behind-the-scenes look at Boston's major paper, the *Boston Globe*, you'll have to plan in advance, and you can't bring kids under 9. You get to see the newsroom (and you thought the kids' rooms were messy!), composing room, and press room. Children might be surprised at how putting together a paper really works. A video before the tour explains a lot.

Jamaica Plain/Roxbury/Dorchester

Franklin Park Zoo

One Franklin Park Road
Boston, MA 02121
(617) 541-LION
www.zoonewengland.com

Franklin Park Zoo

Hours: Apr.-Sep., 10 a.m. - 5 p.m., weekends until 6 p.m. Oct.-Mar., daily 10 a.m. - 4 p.m.

Admission: $7, adults; $4, children 2-15; under 2, free. First Saturday of the month, free admission if you arrive before noon.

Directions: Take the Orange Line to Forest Hills, then catch the number 16 bus. If you are driving, this is one of the few places around Boston that has free, plentiful parking.

The Franklin Park Zoo sits in the 500-acre Franklin Park, part of the Emerald Necklace. On your way to the zoo, don't be surprised to see golfers zipping around in golf carts. There is an 18-hole course in the park as well as a pond and a 100-acre woods (not *the* Hundred Acre Woods, alas). The 72-acre zoo recently got a facelift, making it a much better place to visit. More than 20 new exhibits have been installed here and at its sister zoo, the Stone Zoo in Stoneham.

At Franklin Park Zoo, we first head straight for the Tropical Forest. The highlight of our last visit was seeing a mother gorilla carrying her toddler on her back (sound familiar, anyone?). The Franklin Farm exhibit allows children to pet cows and goats and always gets a thumbs-up. The Butterfly Landing, open only in the summer, has more than 1,000 butterflies to gaze at in wonder (it's an extra $1 for this exhibit). You'll find all the usual suspects, as well— lions, kangaroos, and giraffes. The zoo covers a lot of ground so a stroller or back-pack is a good idea.

Taking a break at the zoo.

Jennifer Bester

Boston by Neighborhood

Jamaica Pond & Boathouse

The Jamaicaway
Boston, MA 02130
(617) 522-6258 (boathouse), (617) 522-4573 (rangers)
www.jamaicaplain.com

Jamaica Pond & Boathouse

Hours: Dawn to Dusk.

Boat rentals: rowboat $8 Boston residents or $10 nonresidents per hour—sailboat, $15/$20.

Directions: Take the Riverway south from Route 9.

Few neighborhood parks are so well-used and well-loved as Jamaica Pond, and for good reason. The grounds are well-maintained, the vibe is relaxed and friendly, and glimpses of nature are everywhere to be enjoyed, right in the middle of a city neighborhood. It also happens to be the site of America's first reservoir and part of the Emerald Necklace. In every season and at just about any daylight hour, the pond's paved trail is occupied by people of all ages and from many walks of life. It's a place to kick back and enjoy the small pleasures of childhood: feeding the ducks and geese; tossing sticks and rocks; spotting a majestic swan, a shy turtle, numerous dogs; walking, running, and riding; having a picnic and meeting old or new friends. (Adults are not allowed to use bikes or in-line skates, except on the outer trail close to the road. Younger children can skate or ride by the pond's bank as long as they are supervised.) Children under five will enjoy just being there. Older kids will be more interested in sledding on the very steep hill just adjacent to the pond or getting out on the water in a rented boat. You can rent sailboats July through Labor Day; rowboats, April through September. Call ahead because weekends are busy. Jamaica Pond also hosts a number of festive but low-key seasonal celebrations. One of the best, (but maybe a little scary for small children), is the Lantern Parade. This is held every year when we push back the clocks. Nothing is more beautiful than seeing hundreds of homemade lanterns glowing in the night as people make their way around the pond.

Feeding the ducks at Jamaica Pond.

Jamaica Plain/Roxbury/Dorchester

John F. Kennedy Library and Museum

**Columbia Point
Dorchester, MA 02125
(877) 616-4599
www.jfklibrary.org**

John F. Kennedy Library and Museum

Hours: daily, 9 a.m. - 5 p.m.; closed Thanksgiving, Christmas, & New Year's Day.

Admission: adults, $8; 13-17, $4; under 12, free; special exhibits extra.

Directions: Take the Red Line to JFK/UMass station; take a free shuttle bus to the library.

This is the place to learn everything you ever wanted to know about JFK. The museum has 25 exhibits detailing his life and presidency. Although much of the museum's content is targeted for adults and older children, most kids can enjoy the mock-up of certain White House rooms. There's the "White House Hall," with rooms off it leading to the "Oval Office" and also a re-creation of his brother Robert F. Kennedy's Justice Department office. A piece of the Berlin Wall is also on display at the library. Jacqueline Kennedy is not neglected; many exhibits show off her interests. As you leave, you'll pass through an atrium, 115 feet high, with fantastic views of Boston, where a gigantic American flag is displayed. The museum café is also a great place to enjoy the same views of the harbor.

Olmsted Park

**Perkins Street
Jamaica Plain, MA 02130**

Olmsted Park

Directions: Take the Riverway south from Route 9.

This namesake park for master planner of the Emerald Necklace, Frederick Law Olmsted, is composed of three ponds, numerous walkways with footbridges, and a bike path. It is between the Jamaica Pond area and the Riverway, both jewels in the necklace. You could meander endlessly throughout the park system. Kids learning to ride their bikes can't ask for a better place to go. This is also a fabulous place to come with older kids to go sledding when it snows. The hills guarantee a wild ride.

Boston by Neighborhood

Best Local Playground

I can't give just one playground for this part of the book because the neighborhoods I include are so far apart. If you are in Dorchester, head over to Castle Island (see entry pg. 72). The zoo has a playground of its own in the unlikely event the kids should tire of the animals. It's right next to the snack bar area, which means you can watch them play while you finish eating. Over in JP, a wonderful Tot Lot for smaller children has more toys than you'll see at any other playground. Residents bring toys and leave them for others to use.

The well-cared-for playground has climbing structures and a sand box. If you are at Jamaica Pond, cross the Jamaicaway (go to the crosswalk!) at Pond Street. Take a right on the parkway. Go one block to Burroughs Street. Go down one block to Brewer Street and you'll see it.

Other Offerings Around Town

Several of the following sites are located in Brookline, which is not a part of Boston, but is nestled right next to it. A large Jewish population makes their home here, which is evident in the many delis and kosher restaurants up and down Harvard Square. The Green Line "C" train will drop you off at Coolidge Corner, the main part of the town. The Larz Anderson Park is a great spot for families. South Boston, or "Southie," often ignored in many guidebooks, does have some charming areas, too. Carson Beach and Castle Island are a lot of fun in the summer. The closest place for real hiking or cross-country skiing is in Milton, at the Blue Hills Reservation. You have 7,000 acres to lose yourself in exploring.

Around Boston

Allandale Farm

259 Allandale Road
Brookline, MA 02467
(617) 524-1531
www.allandalefarm.com

Allandale Farm

Hours: Apr.-Dec., 10 a.m. - 6 p.m.

Admission: free.

Directions: You have to have a car for this one. From Boston, take Route 1 South to the Jamaicaway. Follow the signs for Faulkner Hospital, Dedham and West Roxbury. Turn right at the hospital on Allandale Street.

The last working farm in Boston and Brookline is Allandale Farm, which raises organic fruits and vegetables. At their store, you can buy all sorts of seasonal products from Christmas trees to watermelons. Hayrides in October are fun for kids, and you can sign up for a workshop on making scarecrows ($10). A unique summer camp program is held here from mid-June through mid-August for children ages 4-10. (One week is $275; two weeks is $425.) The three-hour morning camp introduces children to gardening, identifying birds and plants, animals and more. Annually, outdoor sculptures make an appearance at the farm during the Brookline Artists' Open Studios event each spring. This is definitely a great place to show city kids that vegetables don't grow in the grocery store.

Blue Hills Trailside Museum & Reservation

1904 Canton Avenue
Milton, MA 02186
(617) 333-0690
www.massaudubon.org

Blue Hills Trailside Museum & Reservation

Hpurs: Trails—daily, dawn to dusk, all year. Museum—Tues.-Sun., 10 a.m. - 5 p.m.

Admission: adults, $3; children 3-12, $1.50. Mass. Audubon members free.

Directions: Take Rt. 128 (93) from Boston to exit 2B (Milton) to Rt. 138 North. It's a half-mile on the right.

There is enough to do at the almost 7,000-acre reservation to qualify it as a day-trip destination. There are 150 miles of trails to explore, plus the museum, which has exhibits detailing the wildlife you might encounter while hiking around. In my book, however, what is great here are all the various programs offered throughout the year. On weekends, there is story time at 11 a.m. (for ages 3-6), plus the "mystery species" presentation at 1 p.m. (for all ages). At 3 p.m., the "theme of the month" is explored (ages 6 and up). The theme might be "Animal Coverings," "Tracking," or "Bones and Skulls."

Boston by Neighborhood

These are all free with general admission. Other special programs such as "Owl Hootenany" or "Maple Sugar Days" are a blast. You can see owls up close or collect sap in buckets. These programs are extra, but completely worth it. Check out the Mass. Audubon Society's website for other events.

Carson Beach

Day Boulevard
South Boston, MA 02127

You don't have to leave the city to go to the beach. Carson Beach, located near Castle Island, offers swimming, with lifeguards in the summer and really fabulous views. You're not going to mistake it for Cape Cod or anything, but the kids won't care. Sand castles and poking around with sticks is fun on any beach. On a hot, sticky city day, heading down here to cool off can't be beat.

Carson Beach

Directions: Take the Red Line to the JFK/Umass stop. It's a two minute walk. Or driving: from Boston, take Route 3 to the JFK Exit, follow the beach along Day Boulevard.

Castle Island

Day Boulevard
South Boston, MA 02127
(617) 268-5744

Kim Foley MacKinnon

Sweeping views at Castle Island.

First off, don't look for a castle and you're not on an island. Castle Island is just one more place in Boston that does not seem to be named correctly, although to be fair it was once an island, in the 1600s. What is here is Fort Independence, which was built between 1834 and 1851. It doesn't matter what it's

Castle Island

Hours: year-round; tours of the fort on summer weekends only.

Directions: From Boston, take Route 3 to the JFK Exit, follow the beach along Day Boulevard until the end.

called though, this is a great place to have a picnic, Rollerblade, swim, watch the planes fly in and out of Logan, and look out at the harbor. There is also a great Tot Lot where the kids can play. A snack bar offers French fries and frappes. You can also fish from the pier.

Around Boston

Kidport at Logan Airport

Terminal C, Logan Airport
Boston, MA
(617) 561-1600
www.massport.com

Kidport at Logan Airport

Hours: Open if terminal is.

Admission: free.

Directions: Take the Blue Line to the airport. Take a free shuttle bus to Terminal C.

Maybe this sounds like a strange destination. After all, who wants to go to the airport if they can help it? But, hey, if you're already there, this is a lifesaver. And if you don't have to hop a plane, but need an activity sure to please, this is a fun outing for kids, even tiny ones. There's an infant area as well as lots of fun stuff to climb on for the bigger kids. The Kidport is a joint venture by the Massport and The Children's Museum, which means it is more than just an area with a few toys scattered about. Parents beware: you have to pass by a Children's Museum gift shop on the way in.

Larz Anderson Park

Bounded by Newton Street, Avon Street, and Goddard Avenue
Brookline, MA 02146
(617) 730-2069
www.townofbrooklinemass.com

Larz Anderson Park, with 64 acres, has everything one could hope for in a park: an excellent playground, a picnic table area, barbecue pits, a pond, and an outdoor ice-skating rink and sports fields. Don't miss the Temple of Love pavilion on the edge of the lagoon. It's a pleasant spot for sitting. The views of Boston are amazing. In the summer, you can have a fabulous cookout or picnic if you reserve a spot in advance. Come winter, strap on skates and take a whirl on the ice. They usually rig up an area next to the rink where tiny skaters can practice while holding on to plastic milk crates.

Larz Anderson Park

Hours: Fri., 7:30 p.m. - 9:30 p.m.; Sat., noon - 5 & 7:30-9:30 p.m.; Sun., noon - 5 p.m.

Admission: Ice-skating—Dec.-Feb.; Adults, $3, children, $1 (skate rental, $4.40, all ages). Single grill rental—$20 residents; $25 nonresidents. Larger sites and the Temple of Love are also available to rent.

Directions: Take Route 9 west, toward Newton. After you pass the Brookline Reservoir on your left, turn left onto Lee Street and follow to the end. At the light, turn left onto Newton Street. Follow Newton Street for approximately 1/2 mile. The road will fork, go to the left onto Goddard Avenue. Park is 1/2 mile on the right.

Boston by Neighborhood

This park is more a resident pleasure since it is not really accessible by the T. If you are a major car buff, you can visit the Museum of Transportation (see below) and then let the kids run around in the enclosed playground here afterwards.

Museum of Transportation

15 Newton Street, Larz Anderson Park
Brookline, MA 02146
(617) 522-6140
www.mot.org

Museum of Transportation

Hours: Tues.-Sun., 10 a.m. - 5 p.m. and Monday holidays. Closed New Year's Day, Thanksgiving, and Christmas.

Admission: adults, $5; children, 6-18, $3; under 6, free.

Directions: See above directions to Larz Anderson Park.

The centerpiece of the Larz Anderson Park in Brookline is the Museum of Transportation. The core of the museum is the original stable of early automobiles donated to the city of Boston as part of the Larz Anderson estate, housed in the original carriage house. While the rotating exhibits upstairs are strictly off-limits to little fingers, the downstairs is devoted exclusively to the tiny car lovers, and other than a large collection of vintage and rare automobile toys, allows for interaction. There is a pedal kart ride-on carousel; the bridge of a Boston Trolley with bell; continuously running, automobile-related Little Rascals episodes; and coloring supplies on a crafts table. Through spring, summer, and fall, there are also weekly Sunday lawn events with marquee theme days free with museum admission.

Cambridge/Harvard Square

One nickname for Cambridge you might hear bandied about is "Boston's Left Bank." Another is "The People's Republic of Cambridge." This is due to its liberal leanings and independent character. Harvard University and Massachusetts of Technology are the big draws around here. Each square in Cambridge—Harvard, Central, Inman, Kendall, and Porter—has its own charms. If you are new to the city, you'll probably head for Harvard Square first. Since this is more a guidebook

Entertainment is always a thrill in Harvard Square.

Cambridge/Harvard

for the other side of the Charles River, I've touched only on a few favorites, most of them around Harvard Square. Don't be afraid to explore on your own. Cambridge has much to offer.

Harvard Square is a destination by itself, offering endless opportunities for people watching and entertainment, all for free. Any warm night brings out crowds of people, all happy to just hang out. Any number of musicians and performers come out too, which make the square an exciting spot to be. There are so many bookstores in Harvard Square that the tourist board puts out a bookstore guide to help tourists find all 24 of them. In recent years, the individual character of the square has been lost a little as big-name stores have moved in, pushing out independents. I guess that's the price of progress. But the spirit of the area hasn't been diminished. Any visit to Harvard Square is not complete without wandering around the Harvard University Campus, the oldest university in the United States.

Boston by Neighborhood

Curious George Goes to Wordsworth

1 JFK Street, Harvard Square
Cambridge, MA 02138
(617) 498-0062
www.wordsworthkids.com

Right in the heart of Harvard Square is a store begging for your attention. The bright yellow storefront will surely catch yours and your children's eyes as you wander about. Oh, that familiar monkey won't be lost on your kids either. Wordsworth, a wonderful independent bookstore down the block, is the parent of this charming store. Two floors are packed with books and toys that are not to be found at every bookstore. Of course, Curious George books and paraphernalia are everywhere, but by no means is that all. Try to get out of here without buying something. I have yet to do so.

Harvard Museum of Natural History

26 Oxford Street
Cambridge, MA 02138
(617) 495-3045
www.hmnh.harvard.edu

This is one of Boston's hidden treasures. I don't know many locals who have been here, which is too bad, because they are missing out on a unique museum. Located in one rather sprawling structure, the Harvard Museum of Natural History shares the building with the Botanical Museum, the Museum of Comparative Zoology, and the Mineralogical and Geological Museum (admission covers all, plus the Peabody Museum of Archaeology and Ethnology—not always a big kid hit, so it's safe to skip it). Sheer numbers are what get you here: 3,000 glass flowers, a 1,642-pound amethyst, a 42-foot-long prehistoric marine reptile, and so on. The vast amount of taxi-

Don't worry—it's not real. Harvard Museum of Natural History.

Cambridge/Harvard

dermic animals (we call them "statues" for our young animal lover) is unbelievable. It seems that the energetic Harvard ancestors caught one of every creature in the world and displayed it here. They are so lifelike, you might jump when you see the tiger! You'll have to drag the kids away.

Harvard University

26 Oxford Street
Cambridge, MA 02138
(617) 495-1573
www.harvard.edu

Although you can walk through Harvard Yard any time, I recommend going on a tour if you can. The student guides are full of information about the history and architecture of the nation's first university (founded in 1636) and can tell you all about the libraries and museums on campus. They describe the life of a Harvard student and make the place seem a little less intimidating. Funny stories and lore make the tour interesting for older kids. Little ones will probably enjoy people watching and being pushed or carried around as you explore. There are plenty of places to just sit and relax in the shade of a hundreds-years-old tree. Look for the statue of John Harvard, which makes for a good story. The statue, sculpted in 1884, is just an idea of what the artist thought he looked like, as there are no known images of Harvard. Also, the school was founded in 1636, not 1638 and, finally, Harvard was not the founder, he was a benefactor.

If you don't opt for the tour, walk around instead. The university is quite beautiful and surprisingly quiet and peaceful. Don't forget to tell the kids that six U.S. presidents attended Harvard. Maybe they'll get inspired.

Harvard University

Hours: Call ahead.

Admission: Free tours offered during the academic year.

Directions: Take the Red Line to the Harvard Square stop.

Harvard Museum of Natural History

Hours: daily 9 a.m. - 5 p.m. Closed New Year's Day, July 4, Thanksgiving, and Christmas.

Admission: adults, $6.50; children, $4; under 3, free. Free to all Wednesdays, 3-5 p.m. and Sundays, 9 a.m. - noon.

Directions: Take the Red line to Harvard Square. The Museum is located through Harvard Yard. Cross through the Yard and go up Oxford Street. It's the fourth building on the right.

Boston by Neighborhood

Minuteman Bikeway

For the biking family, this is a great and very popular bike path that was once a railroad corridor. It closely follows the path that Paul Revere took on his way to Lexington. Of course, maybe riding with your kids in back or alongside you for 10 miles or so is not your idea of fun. Nobody said you had to do the whole thing! There are many places to take breaks and signs point out nearby restaurants and facilities. You can get on the path in Cambridge, Arlington, Lexington and Bedford. The bikeway runs from the Red Line Alewife Station in Cambridge to Bedford. We usually get on it in Cambridge and stop for lunch in Davis Square. Go to **www.state.ma.us/mhd/paths/bikep.htm** to get a map of the entire route. The bikeway can get a little crowded, though. Remind the kids to stay on the right side of the path and look out for faster bikers. It's a nice, well-maintained path that makes it easy for kids to ride.

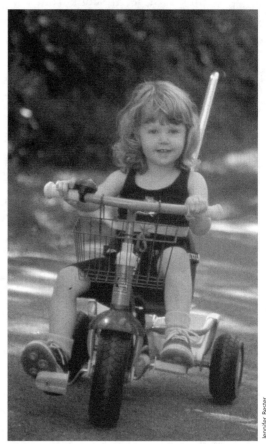

Jennifer Bester

The Minuteman Bikeway is great for leisurely riding.

Cambridge/Harvard

MIT Museum

265 Massachusetts Avenue
Cambridge, MA 02139
(617) 253-4444
www.mit.edu/museum

MIT Museum

Hours: Tues.-Fri., 10 a.m. - 5 p.m.; Sat. & Sun., noon - 5 p.m.

Admission: adults, $5; children 5-18, $2.

Directions: Take the Red Line to the Central Square stop.

The Massachusetts Institute of Technology's museum has the world's largest collection of holography. If your kids have ever gotten any holo-gram cards out of cereal boxes and thought they were cool, wait until they see them here. Holograms are really the tip of the iceberg at this interactive museum, which has all sorts of cutting-edge technology displays. Hands-on is the order of the day here, where kids can watch what the heat of their hands does to the plasma globes. Kids also might like the "Hall of Hacks," where notorious pranks by MIT students are displayed, although you prob-ably don't want to encourage your kids in this direction!

MIT also offers family programs. New themes are introduced each month at the Invention Studio. You might use Twinkies in the "Gastobot" series or use an Etch-a-Sketch in an "Art on the Screen" program. The cost is $25 per adult/child team. Also, on the last Sunday of the month during the school year, from 2-4 p.m., come in for a free (with admission) program on science given by staff and students. You'll work on a project related to something going on at the school. Prove to your kids that science can be fun!

To learn more about MIT itself, take a tour of the campus. Like Harvard, stu-dents give the tours and love to tell anecdotes. Call (617) 253-4795. The museum gift shop is another great place to pick up unusual gifts and souvenirs.

Boston by Neighborhood

Mount Auburn Cemetery

580 Mt. Auburn Street
Cambridge, MA 02138
(617) 547-7105

Mount Auburn Cemetery
Directions: Take the Red Line to Harvard Square.

This attractive 174-acre cemetery makes for a beautiful and peaceful walk, even with kids in tow. It was the first garden cemetery in the U.S. and was landscaped as an arboretum. Henry Wadsworth Longfellow and other notables are buried here. From the tower on the grounds you have a 360-degree view of the surrounding area. Pick up a walking-tour pamphlet at the gatehouse that has a map of famous graves as well as descriptions of flora and fauna. You can take in a little history while the kids stretch their legs.

Best Local Playground— Cambridge Common

At the juncture of Massachusetts Avenue and Garden Street, your kids can play where once the Continental Army trained. The large playground, complete with swings and tons of structures to climb on, is a couple of blocks from Harvard Square, but well worth seeking out. There is a picnic table and the playground is enclosed. Look for the Civil War monument and another in remembrance of the Irish famine.

3 Trails and Tours

Sightseeing with a Purpose

Boston has a trail or a tour for just about everything. From a historical perspective of colonial America to even more specialized tours, such as literary, women's history, black heritage, or a hunt for the solar system modeled here on earth, you should be able to find a tour to interest the whole family. Some of the trails are probably too long for smaller kids, so just be creative and tailor the walks to suit your family. Older children might be able to connect a trail and its sights to a school project. You can also make it fun for the kids if you pose it as a treasure hunt. Arranged tours on a bus or a duck boat (more on that later!) are wonderful if walking is not your thing. Hopping on and off a bus may appeal to you for the chance to rest in between sightseeing and let someone else tell you about the sites.

Many of the individual places on the trails are listed under their specific Boston location in the previous chapter. If you want more info, such as times and prices, look in the index for the exact page on which it can be found.

A Parent's Guide to Boston

Trails and Tours

On the Trail of...
The Freedom Trail

The Freedom Trail

North
West ◆ East
South

BUNKER HILL MEMORIAL

City Square

USS Constitution

Copp's Hill Burial Ground

Old North Church

Paul Revere House

Faneuil Hall/ Quincy Market

King's Chapel & Burying Ground

Boston Massacre Site / Old State House

Benjamin Franklin Statue

Old Corner Bookstore

Massachusetts State House

Old South Meeting House

Visitor's Center

BOSTON COMMON

PUBLIC GARDENS

Trails and Tours

This is the most famous of all the Boston trails. Follow the red painted line, about 2.5 miles long, for a tour of 16 sites from the Colonial and Revolutionary era. Most sites are free, but a few do charge an admission. Start off at the Boston Common Visitor Information Center, near the Park Street stop, where you can pick up a copy of the trail sites and any other information you might need. To see everything properly, you'll need more than a day. Pick and choose what is most important to your family and skip the rest. Visit **www.thefreedomtrail.org**. for a virtual tour. Shorter tours are given by the National Park Service ((617) 242-5642; **www.nps.gov**) April-November, which visit most, but not all, of the sites. They also have a few additional sites, which differ from the Freedom Trail (ask about the Junior Ranger program). Tours start at the Boston National Historic Park Visitor Center across from the Old State House.

1 Boston Common (see pg. 17)

The Common is bordered by Tremont, Boylston, and Beacon Streets. Once a cattle grazing field, now a public park smack dab in the middle of the city.

2 Massachusetts State House (see pg. 21)

Beacon Street. The beautiful gold-domed State House is the oldest building on Beacon Hill.

3 Park Street Church (see pg. 26)

One Park St. Founded in 1809.

4 Granary Burying Ground (see pg. 26)

Tremont St., next to the Park Street Church. Samuel Adams, Paul Revere, and John Hancock are buried here.

Massachusetts State house

Trails and Tours

5 *King's Chapel & Burying Ground (see pg. 20)*

Corner of Tremont and School Streets. Nobody would sell the British governor land to build a non-Puritan church in 1688, so he built one on the town burying ground. So there.

6 *Site of the First Public School & Ben Franklin Statue (see pg. 16)*

School St. The school (Boston Latin) has since moved, but a plaque and statue of Franklin show where the country's first public school opened.

7 *Old Corner Bookstore (see pg. 24)*

One School Street. Literary gathering place and publishing house.

8 *Old South Meeting House (see pg. 24)*

310 Washington Street. A meeting here in 1773 set off that famous Boston Tea Party.

9 *Old State House (see pg. 25)*

Corner of State and Washington Streets. The Declaration of Independence was first read from the Old State House balcony, the oldest surviving public building in Boston.

10 *Boston Massacre Site (see pg. 19)*

Next to the Old State House. Look for the ring of cobblestones on a traffic island where this incident occurred.

11 *Faneuil Hall (see pg. 47)*

Merchants Row. Many meetings in this 250-year-old hall determined the course of history.

12 *Paul Revere House (see pg. 60)*

19 North Square.

Paul Revere House

Trails and Tours

13 Old North Church (see pg. 59)

193 Salem Street. The two lanterns signaling the British were coming hung from this church's steeple in 1775.

14 Copp's Hill Burial Ground (see pg. 58)

Uphill from the Old North Church. Sexton Robert Newman, who hung the famous lanterns in the Old North Church, is buried here.

15 USS Constitution (see pg. 64)

Pier 1, Charlestown. Also known as "Old Ironsides," it is the oldest commissioned warship afloat.

16 Bunker Hill Monument (see pg. 63)

Monument Square, Charlestown. A monument marking the site of the first major battle of the American Revolution.

Trails and Tours

Community Solar System Hunt

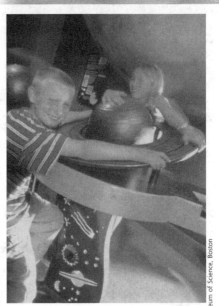

This is great fun and can give your kids a sense of scale in the big scheme of things. It's a treasure hunt of the solar system, sponsored by the Museum of Science as part of its "Welcome to the Universe" exhibit. The "Sun" is located at the museum and the planets are placed at accurate proportions throughout the city. The scale is 400 million to 1! An inch equals 6,215 miles.

To start off, get a "Community Solar System Passport," either on-line at **www.mos.org** or at the museum. Track down the planets and do a pencil rubbing of the planet's symbol, found on the sculpture, on the correct page of the passport. When finished, send it to the museum and they'll send you a certificate of completion. The passport has directions to each of the "planets" as well as fun facts. They can all be reached by public transportation, but be warned, a couple are out of the city.

Looking for the planets.

Museum of Science, Boston

Mail your passport to:
Community Solar System,
Charles Hayden Planetarium,
Science Park,
Boston, MA, 02114.
Call (617) 723-2500 or
visit **www.mos.org**.
if you need more info.

Trails and Tours

1 Sun
In the Museum of Science's "Welcome to the Universe" exhibit.

2 Mercury
In the Museum of Science, in the front plaza.

3 Venus
In the Museum of Science, on the roof of the garage near the Gilliland Observatory.

4 Earth
Royal Sonesta Hotel, on the brick walkway in the courtyard.

5 Mars
Cambridgeside Galleria Mall, 2nd floor balcony, in front of elevators.

6 Jupiter
South Station, in the Grand Concourse near the food court.

7 Saturn
Cambridge Public Library, in the Anthony J. DeVito Music Room.

8 Uranus
Jamaica Plain Branch of the Boston Public Library, in the entryway, near the periodicals.

9 Neptune
Square One Mall, Saugus, in the food court.

10 Pluto
Riverside Station, Newton, on the train platform.

Trails and Tours

Big Dig Tour or "The CA/T Walk"

Massachusetts Turnpike Authority
Central Artery/Tunnel Authority
185 Kneeland Street
Boston, MA 02111
(617) 951-6400
www.bigdig.com

This is a self-guided walking tour of the Big Dig as recommended by the Massachusetts Turnpike Authority. A guided tour is planned for spring 2002. Call for details. As this is an evolving project, I highly recommend calling or checking on the website before visiting. Things change all the time. You can get a walking tour map booklet with more details sent to you via e-mail or faxed to you. If you don't feel like doing the whole tour, take a look at the seven sites below anyway. You might be nearby a site while en route to somewhere else. The Big Dig truly is an amazing project.

Here is the tour as it stands now. I have given detailed directions since you need to be looking from specific spots to see the work in progress. No hardhat needed.

Trails and Tours

1 *South Station Bus Terminal*
Take the Red Line to South Station. Follow signs to the bus terminal. Look out from the glass-enclosed staircase on the second floor of the terminal. Workers are building 2,000 feet of a new underground highway. This is part of the Big Dig's largest tunnel construction.

2 *A Street/Mt. Washington Avenue*
From the bus terminal, head back to the South Station Commuter Rail and Amtrak platforms. Enter the concourse area and exit through Summer Street doors. Go down Summer Street, cross the Fort Point Channel on the Summer Street Bridge and take your first right on Melcher St. Follow to the end and take a right on A Street. Stay on the pedestrian walkway. After you pass a tall sound barrier wall, take a right on Mt. Washington Avenue. Here you'll see a construction area where crews are building an eight-lane highway under the Fort Point Channel. This is a very tricky part of the project because of bad soil conditions and its proximity to the Red Line.

3 *Summer Street/Congress Street Kiosk*
Go back to A Street, following the pedestrian walkways to view the South Boston tunnel construction to the right of A Street. Then follow Summer Street to Congress Street where you can stop on the bridge at an info kiosk.

4 *Dewey Square/Atlantic Avenue*
Go back to South Station and pass by the front. Here are Plexiglas windows to look through at what will be the deepest point under Dewey Point, 120 feet below the Red Line. Cross Summer Street and go north on Atlantic Avenue. You'll come to Vent Building #3, under construction between Congress St. and Northern Ave. The vent building will supply fresh air to the tunnels and remove exhaust.

Trails and Tours

5 *Surface Artery*

High Street to State Street. Continue down Atlantic Ave. to the Boston Harbor Hotel. Cross Atlantic Ave. onto Surface Artery. You are directly below the elevated highway. Underneath your feet construction is ongoing to build the underground highway.

6 *Haymarket*

Continue on Surface Artery north and take a left into Marketplace Center. Take a right in front of Quincy Market. Go straight to Clinton Street at the Dock Square Parking Garage. Follow Clinton to the end and take a right onto North Street. Follow signs to the North End. Take a left before the elevated artery. Go through the Haymarket vendors and look for the large Freedom Trail sign. Take the passageway under the Central Artery, and you'll find more Plexiglas windows to check out the tunnel construction.

7 *MDC Charles River Dam*

Keep on the passageway and cross over Cross Street. Bear right on Endicott Street and then take a left on Stillman Place. Take a right on North Washington Street and go three blocks to the Causeway Street intersection. Cross Causeway St. and go left. Go right on Beverly Street and look for signs to Lovejoy Wharf. Pass the wharf and enter the MDC Charles River Dam pedestrian walkway. Follow until you get to the Paul Revere Landing Park in Charlestown, one of the new parks created during the project. In 2003, the old I-93 above you will be gone.

Trails and Tours

Black Heritage Trail

As the name states, this is a trail tracing the history of African Americans who settled in this area of Beacon Hill between 1800 and 1900. Like the Freedom Trail, it starts at Boston Common. Call the Boston African American National Historic Site for more info at (617) 742-5415.

Trails and Tours

1 ***Robert Gould Shaw & 54th Regiment Memorial***
At the entrance to Boston Common at Park and Beacon Streets. Honors the service of African Americans in the Civil War. Shaw, who was white, volunteered to lead the first black regiment in the North.

2 ***George Middleton House***
5 Pinckney Street. Oldest home built by a black person on Beacon Hill and home of George Middleton, a colonel in the American Revolution.

3 ***Phillips School***
Corner of Anderson and Pinckney Streets. One of the first Boston public schools to admit blacks.

4 ***John J. Smith home***
86 Pinckney Street. A black abolitionist center and runaway slave meeting place.

5 ***Charles Street Meeting House***
Mt. Vernon and Charles Streets. Frederick Douglass, Soujourner Truth, and Wendall Phillips all spoke here.

6 ***Lewis & Harriet Hayden House***
66 Phillips Street. An Underground Railroad stop for runaway slaves. Lewis Hayden served in the State Legislature in 1873.

7 ***Coburn's Gaming House***
Phillips and Irving Streets.

8-12 ***Smith Court Residences***
Homes typical of black residents in the 1800s.

13 ***Abiel Smith School***
46 Joy Street. A grammar school built in 1834 for black students. Later it was boycotted because of segregation.

14 ***African Meeting House***
8 Smith Court. The oldest black church building in the U.S.

Trails and Tours

Guided Tours

Don't be confused by the names of these tours, for they are tours, even if they're called trails. You will pay money, and people will drive you around town telling you all sorts of things you never knew. A couple of them even take you into the harbor or way out of town, making them more than run-of-the-mill tours. I've included the ones that I think are of special interest to families. There are dozens and dozens of tours around, so make sure you know what you are paying for before you go.

Boston by Little Feet

77 North Washington Street
Boston, MA 02114
(617) 367-2345
www.bostonbyfoot.com

Older kids bored by regular tours geared more for adults might enjoy Boston by Little Feet. Targeted for kids ages six-12, the guides make history fun and adventurous. The tour is a shorter version of the Freedom Trail, and kids are invited to answer such questions as "Why is it nick-named the French Wedding Cake?" and "More people visit me than Disney World. True or False?" Take the tour to find out the answers. Adults will enjoy it too.

> **Boston by Little Feet**
>
> When: May-October, Saturdays and Mondays at 10 a.m.; Sundays at 2 p.m.
>
> Tickets: adults, $8; children 6-12, $6; children must be accompanied by an adult.
>
> Where: Meet in front of Faneuil Hall, at the statue of Samuel Adams.

Trails and Tours

Boston Duck Tours

Administration Office
790 Boylston Street, MA 02199
(617) 723-DUCK
www.bostonducktours.com

If you have spent any time in Boston, you'll have noticed the brightly colored odd-looking bus/boats around town. People may have been making funny noises at you, and the driver may have been wearing something odd on his head, like a Viking hat. The "buses" are retired WWII amphibious vehicles reincarnated as tour buses. They were used to move soldiers and supplies from ships to beachheads in Europe. Now they are used to move tourists around in style, in and out of the water. Every conDUCKtor (get it?) assumes a different character complete with personality. Your driver might be a Viking or the artist, Vincent Van Duck. The big draw of the tour is when you leave land behind and splash into the Charles River. All the children on board are allowed to steer for a while in the water. Kids will be interested to know that area schoolchildren named the various Ducks. You may take a ride in Back Bay Bertha, North End Norma, or Beantown Betty.

Quack your way through town on a Boston Duck Tour.

Trails and Tours

The tour hits all the expected tourist sites. Somehow, it just seems a little more fun when the driver hits the horn and everyone on board quacks at pedestrians. The entire tour is 80 minutes long, which might make it too long for smaller children. It runs ran or shine. There is a canopy, and the Ducks are heated. Bundle up in cold weather. It can get chilly on the Charles River. Tickets sell out fast in the summer so it's wise to line up early, as reservations are not taken. A nice touch is that you can stow strollers in a safe place by the buses.

Boston History Collaborative

175 Berkeley Street, 3E
Boston, MA 02117
(617) 574-5950

> **Boston History Collaborative**
>
> Call for hours and dates of each tour. They vary and some are given only in the warmer months.

The Boston History Collaborative offers a more in-depth look at different aspects of Boston and its history. Any of the following tours designed by them can be guided tours, or you can do it yourself if you get their materials, usually for a fee. Their website also spells out all the sites on the tours. If you are looking for more than just surface information about Boston, these tours are designed for you.

Trails and Tours

Boston by Sea – Maritime Trail

www.bostonbysea.org

Take a 90-minute ride around the Boston Harbor and enjoy the performance of costumed actors belting out tunes about Boston's interaction with the sea. The kids will love learning sea shanties (all

> **Boston by Sea – Maritime Trail**
>
> Cost: Adults, $25; children under 12, $10.
>
> Where: Leaves from Long Wharf

clean, don't worry). Although it may seem a little goofy, music and costumes get the kids hooked every time. Besides, as long as they get all the facts straight, which they do, why shouldn't learning be fun?

Another option is a free 25-minute guided tour of Long Wharf, also with actors in period costume, sure to interest the kids. This tour leaves from the Marriott Custom House on Lower State Street. You can also conduct your own tour. Visit the website for detailed maps. A few sites you'll visit include Long Wharf, historic piers, and the Charlestown Navy Yard.

Literary Trail of Greater Boston

www.lit-trail.org

This trail/tour, whatever, is for the book-loving kids in your family, the older ones. It's worth the steep price if your family has a love of literature. The guided tour (transportation provided) starts at the Omni Parker House, where many literati dined and debated, then

> **Literary Trail of Greater Boston**
>
> When: Saturdays at 9 a.m. (Tours last 3.5 hours.)
>
> Cost: adults, $35; students, $29.
>
> Where: Omni Public House

you're off to visit the Boston Public Library, America's first free municipal library. After that, it's on to Concord to see Emerson's private study; Orchard House, home to Louisa May Alcott; and Thoreau's Walden Pond. You can end the tour in Harvard Square, America's first college, or head back for lunch at the Parker House.

Trails and Tours

Self-guided tour

Self-guided tour

Price: $19.

For do-it-yourselfers, you can pay a $19 fee and get the guidebook "The Literary Trail of Greater Boston," by Susan Wilson and the Boston History Collaborative, plus free admission to the Gibson House in Boston and the Orchard House and the Concord Museum in Concord. This is a little easier on the pocketbook than the guided tour, but obviously, you'll need a car.

Innovation Odyssey

www.innovationodyssey.com

Innovation Odyssey

When: Saturdays at 2 p.m.

Cost: $25 for adults; $15 for children under 13.

Where: Leaves from 28 State Street/Citizens' Bank

Directions: Take the Orange or Blue Line to State Street.

This tour is recommended for kids over 10. It's a fascinating look at inventors and sights in Boston where many important discoveries were made. The two-hour tour takes you to Harvard University, Massachusetts Institute of Technology, and what's called "Genetown, USA," (the center of gene research). You'll see just where Alexander Graham Bell invented the telephone and where modern surgery started at Massachusetts General Hospital. Actors keep things moving along, while teaching you about history.

Trails and Tours

Historic Neighborhoods

99 Bedford Street
Boston, MA 02111
(617) 426-1885
www.historic-neighborhoods.org

This is yet another fabulous organization that makes exploring Boston and its history a pleasure. Programs include Neighborhood Discovery Walks, Urban Explorer Series, and Ducklings Day Parade. Although these activities may be more interesting or convenient to those who live here, anyone who wants to explore more of Boston than a quick jaunt through town can give you should check out the Neighborhood Discovery Tours. Planning is a little tough since the tours are periodic, but call ahead to see what's offered. Recent ones explored Mission Hill and Hyde Park.

HN is the host of the annual Ducklings Days Parade held on Mother's Day, a not-to-miss event if you have young children familiar with the *Make Way for Ducklings* book by Robert McCloskey. This may sound silly, but children dress up in their favorite duck outfits and quack their way through Beacon Hill—and they've done it annually since 1979. If you want to march in the parade, you have to register ($15 in advance; $20 day of).

Trails and Tours

Old Town Trolleys

**7 Commercial Wharf
Boston, MA 02110
(617) 269-7010
www.trolleytours.com**

Old Town Trolleys
Cost: adults, $23; children 4-12, $10.

Old Town Trolley Tours of Boston

The Trolley is an easy way to see the city.

Hopping on and off the Old Town Trolley is a convenient and easy way to see the city. Sixteen stops hit all the major tourist areas and save you driving and parking. A complete tour without getting off is about two hours. Don't expect much more than an overview of the city. Of course, children love to ride in trolleys, and the drivers are all full of lore and funny stories. This is the tour to take if you want to explore parts of the Freedom Trail without wearing out your shoes. There's not a lot of space for strollers, which must be folded up. Try to leave it home or at your hotel if you can.

Trails and Tours

Women's Heritage Trail

22 Holbrook Street
Boston, MA 02130
(617) 522-2872
www.bwht.org

The Boston Women's Heritage Trail organization grew up out of a program in the public schools. Now it sells a guidebook listing all the sites where women made a difference in Boston, as well as publishing many self-guided walking tour brochures. Some of the tours are designed and researched with classes of students from the Boston Public Schools.

Go to their website and print up a walk that interests you. Wherever you are in Boston, you can be sure a woman made her mark nearby. A couple examples of walks include, "Walk Her Walk," a tour designed by fifth-graders. This tour visits sites in Charlestown and the students even protested at the Bunker Hill Monument because of the omission of an important woman's name, Sarah Josepha Hale, on the timeline display. Hale helped raise the necessary money to finish construction of the monument in 1840, but somehow was not acknowledged. She also wrote "Mary Had a Little Lamb." The "Downtown Walk" brings you by the statue of Mary Dyer in front of the State House. Dyer, a Quaker, was hanged in 1660 on Boston Common (not always such a peaceful place) for her religious views.

You'll never have enough time to take in all the sites, but it's worth doing a little research or buying the guidebook to teach your children about the contributions that women made that were often overlooked. At the very least, you can show off while you are sightseeing. Point out where Fannie Farmer published her first cookbook in 1896 (Boston Cooking School, 174 Tremont Street), or where the woman who started "Mother's Day" once lived (15 Pinckney Street.). That woman was Julia Ward Howe. She also wrote the "Battle Hymn of the Republic."

4 All The World's A Stage

Theatres & Music

Boston bends over backwards to interest and include children in the fine arts. Almost every venue in town offers special productions, tours, and programs with a young audience in mind. Productions are often during the day and much cheaper than regular theatre tickets. And let's face it. If you are a busy parent, you probably don't get to the theatre that much. Taking your kids is a way to expose them to something more enriching than TV, and you get to experience some highbrow culture again. Everybody wins. An added bonus is that some of Boston's theatres, such as the Wang and the Shubert, are stunningly gorgeous. They are extravagant with gold and ornate decorations that children can appreciate as much as adults.

Theatres & Music

Theatres

North
West ◄●► East
South

Charles River

Boston Children's Theatre

The Wang Center for the Performing Arts

Once Upon A Time's Interactive Nutcracker

Coolidge Corner Movie Theatre

Wheelock Family Theatre

Boston Symphony Orchestra/ Boston Pops

Boston Ballet

Puppet Showtime Theatre

I've listed only shows and events with children specifically in mind. What this sometimes means is that it's a matinee when the adults in the audience know not to expect utter silence. Remember, you can always just leave if it's too hard for your children to sit still. Before you go, tell your kids about the need to whisper if they just have to talk. If you are going to a play, explain the story in detail and what is going to happen. My three-year-old daughter mistakenly thought she was going to dance in *The Nutcracker*, not just see it! It's helpful for children to know what to expect every step of the way.

For more details, call the theatre, or visit each venue's website.

THEATRE TIP: Call ahead to the box office and ask if booster seats are allowed. This will save you having a squirming child (who can't see over the tall person in front of her) in your lap for two hours while you sullenly stare at the empty space next to you now serving as an expensive coat rack.

Theatres & Music

Boston Ballet

19 Clarendon Street (headquarters; performances are usually at the Wang Center)
Boston, MA 02116
(617) 695-6950
www.bostonballet.org

Boston Ballet

Tickets: $14-65.

Directions: Wang Center—take the Green Line to the Boylston Street stop.

Boston Ballet's most widely seen show, performed at the Wang Center, is *The Nutcracker*, which has an annual six-week run. More than 140,000 people attend the ever-popular classic and with good reason. The beauty of the Wang combined with a Sugar Plum fairy is a magical combination. Many local aspiring child dancers from Boston Ballet's Center for Dance Education appear in the production, adding even more charm. One might think that the show would be more of a draw for young girls and their families, but when we went, both boys and girls were decked in their holiday best, equally thrilled. The ballet is a solid two-and-a-half hours, so if you have a squirmer, think twice. Other fairy tales, such as *Sleeping Beauty* and *Cinderella*, make ballet appealing to a young audience.

Boston Ballet's Nutcracker.

Jennifer W. Lester

Boston Children's Theatre

The Copley Theatre
225 Clarendon Street
Boston, MA 02116
(617) 424-6634
www.bostonchildrenstheatre.org

Boston Children's Theatre

Directions: Take the Green Line to the Copley Square stop.

"Live Theatre for Children by Children" is the motto of Boston Children's Theatre (BCT), a 75-year-old institution. Students in grades 4-12 perform productions such as *Annie*, *The Wizard of Oz*, and *The House at Pooh Corner*. The BCT also offers classes to students in grades K-12. Performances are geared to ages four and up. Most children are natural performers and getting a chance to watch their peers in action often fascinates them.

Theatres & Music

Boston Symphony Orchestra/ Boston Pops Orchestra

**Symphony Hall, 301 Massachusetts Avenue
Boston, MA 02115
(617) 266-1492
www.bso.org**

**Boston Symphony Orchestra/
Boston Pops Orchestra**

Family & youth concerts:
November-April.

Admission: $10; tickets often sell
out in advance.

Directions: Take the Green Line
to the Symphony Hall stop.

The Boston Symphony Youth and Family Concerts, held November through April, are a fabulous introduction to the symphony for children. These concerts are also a bargain for music-loving parents. The Youth Concerts are geared for kids over eight or so and are held weekdays, making it easy for schools to take field trips. The Family Concerts are held Saturdays at 10 a.m. and noon and are for ages five and up. (Children four and under will not be admitted at any time.) The music is chosen with the young audience in mind.

If you attend the 10 a.m. concert, you can come in early for an instrument demonstration by the symphony musicians at 9 a.m. After the later performance, tours of Symphony Hall are given. Either of these choices makes the experience a little more hands-on and interesting for children. Youthful Keith Lockhart, besides being the Boston Pops conductor, is also conductor of the Youth Concerts. His presence alone has brought a lot of interest in recent years to the symphony.

Christian Steine

The Boston Symphony Orchestra at Symphony Hall has family days.

Theatres & Music

Coolidge Corner Movie Theatre (Children's Programs)

290 Harvard Street
Brookline, MA 02445
(617) 734-2531
www.coolidge.org

Coolidge Corner Movie Theatre (Children's Programs)

Hours: Saturday mornings at 10:30 a.m.; Sunday benefit programs at 1 p.m. Call for program details and exact dates.

Admission: live shows are $8; cartoons, $3. Six shows are $35. The Sunday benefits are $10 for adults; $8 for kids.

Directions: Take the Green Line C train to the Cleveland Circle stop.

The Coolidge, Boston's only remaining open Art Deco movie theatre, which is also non-profit, offers a nice change of pace from regular Saturday morning cartoons at home. Every Saturday at 10:30 a.m., a family variety show is offered, and it is not restricted to movies. Magic, dance, puppets, and classic cartoons are all part of the mix. In fact, the Puppet Showplace Theatre (see below) collaborates with the theatre to produce much of the entertainment. As you enter the lobby, look for the giant "Cool Bunny" on hand to greet you through the sea of bubbles produced by a bubble-making machine. Before the main production, local kids perform anything from vaudeville to songs, sort of like a mini-talent show. There are contests, giveaways, and games. A live ensemble plays tunes kids will recognize, such as songs from Disney movies. The main live show along with classic cartoons is reminiscent of the way movies used to be presented. The program is a full 90 minutes with a 10-minute intermission.

Their newest program is called "CoolPOP," which stands for Coolidge Performers Outreach Program. These Sunday performances benefit such organizations as The Brookline Youth Fund and the Bridge Over Troubled Waters. As we went to press, these were monthly shows scheduled for the first Sunday of every month. One was a Tap Caberet, another a Girls Choir. Call for details.

Theatres & Music

Once Upon a Time's Interactive Nutcracker

The Lyric Stage
140 Clarendon St.
Boston MA 02116
(617) 437-7172
www.lyricstage.com

Once Upon a Time's Interactive Nutcracker

Tickets: $7 (children under 2, free), reservations recommended.

Directions: Take the Orange Line to Back Bay or the Green Line to Copley Square.

In this children's interactive version of the Christmas ballet *The Nutcracker*, kids are free to tramp about the set before the show, then a few dozen are chosen to put on costumes and play the whimsical characters while three adult actors narrate and orchestrate. (Note: come early if you want your little star to have a chance to be selected.) This isn't as much pressure as you might think. The young actors are free to simply stand in costume looking cute, and anything they say or do off the cuff just makes the show more entertaining. Likewise, toddlers are free to squirm in the aisles, and anyone and everyone can respond and participate as the show goes on. The concept is brilliant: take a holiday classic that appeals to children but tries the attention span of most of them, and fashion it into something accessible, fun, and—most importantly— brief. Once Upon A Time's execution was somewhat less so, especially in its use of music. Tchaikovsky's magical and familiar score was barely featured, and the adult actors didn't have voices that quite carried, especially given the general bedlam in the room. But the kids won't mind. Overall, this is a wonderful introduction to theater for the youngest viewers (2-8). Once Upon a Time features a new interactive play every month.

Theatres & Music

Puppet Showplace Theatre

32 Station Street
Brookline, MA 02445
(617) 731-6400
www.puppetshowplace.org

Puppet Showplace Theatre

Hours: Performances during the school year are held Saturday & Sunday at 1 p.m. & 3 p.m., with a preschool show on Thursdays at 10:30 a.m.; summer shows are usually held Wednesdays & Thursdays. During school breaks, there are shows daily.

Admission: $8 per person for Family Shows.

Directions: Take the Green Line D to Brookline Village. The theatre is across the street.

The Puppet Showplace Theatre is a magical experience, but make sure you're kids are up for it. Many smaller children are afraid of puppets. Weekend shows are for five-year-olds and older. Special "Tot" shows on Thursdays are targeted for the three-to-five year old set, where the puppeteers introduce themselves and the stories are more familiar.

The theatre is small, with less than 100 seats, so no seat is bad, but make sure you get one by reserving well in advance. Tickets sell out all the time. A recent lineup of shows included "Tom Thumb," "Eeore's Birthday," and "Rumplestiltskin." Sometimes after the shows, the puppeteers will allow children a closer look at the puppets and sometimes (for a fee) you can make your own.

Theatres & Music

The Wang Center for the Performing Arts

270 Tremont Street
Boston, MA 02116
(617) 482-9393
www.wangcenter.org

The Wang Center for the Performing Arts

Directions: Take the Green Line to the Boylston Street stop.

The Wang Center, considered New England's "grand dame" of theatre, opened in 1925. Just visiting the Wang alone is almost worth the price of admission. It was modeled after the Paris Opera Comique and is simply stunning. Murals, gold leaf, marble columns, and intricate carvings make it a feast for the eyes. It is the perfect setting for the Boston Ballet's *The Nutcracker*, held here every year. But guess what? You can also bring the children to see shows such as *Scooby Doo: Stage Fright* and *Blues Clues Live Two!* The Wang offers everything from these obvious children's hits to musicals, dances, concerts, and a classic film series in the winter.

Wheelock Family Theatre

180 The Riverway (Wheelock College)
Boston, MA 02215
(617) 734-4760
www.wheelock.edu

The non-profit Wheelock Family Theatre focuses on shows that everyone can enjoy. Past productions include *The Hobbit, The Prince and the Pauper,* and *The Trumpet and the Swan.* The theatre works hard to attract all ages and offers one drama for adults annually, as well as a musical, and a show for both children and adults. Classes for preschoolers on up include dance, beginning Shakespeare, puppetry and drama, and much more.

Wheelock Family Theatre

Tickets $10-17.

Three mainstage productions annually.

Directions: Take the Green Line D train to the Fenway stop. It's a five-minute walk.

5

Top Picks for Food and Accommodations

A comprehensive listing of restaurants and hotels in the Boston area is beyond the scope of this guide. Since this is a parent-oriented guidebook, I've tried to search out special deals and fun places that have children in mind, or at least places where the staff won't recoil with horror when you walk in the door. Here's a list of 10 restaurants and five hotels where being a kid or having a kid is not considered a liability. They are in no special order of preference. I've just listed them alphabetically.

Food and Accommodations

Redbones

Full Moon

CAMBRIDGE

SOMERVILLE

SOMERVILLE AV

CHELSEA

CHARLESTOWN

EAST BOSTON

HURON AV

BROADWAY AV

MASSACHUSETTS ST

Johnny's Luncheonette

BROOKLINE ST

Union Oyster House

Hyatt Regency Cambridge

Durgin Park
Quincy Market

BOSTON

Boston Harbor Hotel

Le Meridien

STORROW MEMORIAL DR

COMMONWEALTH AV

HARVARD ST

BROOKLINE ST

93

90

Marche Movenpick

The Colonnade

BROOKLINE

Best Western Boston

Midtown Hotel

Food & Lodging

North

West ◄◆► **East**

South

HUNTINGTON AV

TREMONT ST

Tremont 647

JAMAICA PLAIN

ROXBURY

DORCHESTER

Bella Luna/ Milky Way

CYPRESS ST

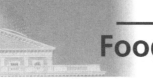

Food and Accommodations

Family-Friendly Restaurants

"Family-friendly" dining can mean different things to different people. To me, it means a place where the whole family can find something enjoyable about the experience. It is not a place where the parents suffer in silence in a theme-oriented restaurant with dressed up characters and video games (although these do have their place) just for the sake of eating out with the kids. It is also not a place where, should your child decide he'd prefer dining under the table rather than with you, the other patrons would give you the evil eye. The following restaurants have good food and interesting atmospheres or histories that everyone should like.

Bella Luna/Milky Way

403 Centre Street
Jamaica Plain, MA 02130
(617) 524-5050

Bowling and pizza. Fun for the whole family! Ah, but this is no regular bowling alley. Gourmet pizza upstairs in the restaurant Bella Luna and candlepin bowling (smaller pins and balls with no

Bella Luna/Milky Way

Hours:
Mon.-Wed. 11 a.m. - 3 p.m.; 5 p.m. - 10 p.m.,
Thu.-Fri. 11 a.m. - 3 p.m.; 5 p.m. - 11 p.m.,
Sat. 11 a.m. - 11 p.m.,
Sun. 10 a.m. - 10 p.m.

holes if you've never done this) downstairs in the Milky Way lounge. You can also eat downstairs in the bar area before bowling. Pizza is served on plastic plates that were decorated by kids. You know the ones. You probably did this as a kid or have done it with your own kids. The bar area is awash with funky lights and solar system sculptures. It's not very smoky, which is a big bonus for a bar. I had my 30th birthday party here, with many children accompanying parents, and we all had a blast. There are ball ramps to put in the alley so kids can definitely knock down some pins. Private parties are common on the weekends so call ahead if you want to bowl.

Food and Accommodations

Durgin Park

**340 Faneuil Hall Marketplace
Boston, MA 02109
(617) 227-2038**

Durgin Park

Hours: daily 11:30 a.m. - 10 p.m.;
Fri. & Sat. until 10:30 p.m.

Directions: Take the Green Line to
Government Center. Cross City Hall
Plaza.

No guidebook would be complete without including Durgin Park. This restaurant, open since 1827, is one of the last places in town to get Indian pudding and true Boston baked beans. It is always busy and packed with tourists. Kids like sitting at the picnic tables. The portions are huge and prices are cheap, so this is good bet for a decent family meal. Just don't look for anyone to hold your hand here—the waitstaff is not known for its friendliness. It's almost a point of pride.

Johnny's Luncheonette

**Harvard Square
1105 Massachusetts Avenue
Cambridge, MA 02138
(617) 495-0055**

Johnny's Luncheonette

Hours: 8 a.m. - 10 p.m.

Directions: Take the Red Line to Harvard Square.

This re-creation of a 50s diner is a much better choice than nearby chains or fast food in Harvard Square. Right on the menu it states, "We love kids," (although it also says to take them outside if they are uncontrollable!). That shouldn't be a problem though. When you sit down, the waitstaff presents a toy to keep kids busy until the food comes. Old-fashioned frappes (milkshakes, for those not familiar with the term) are huge and delicious. Obviously, burgers are big here and the sweet potato fries are outstanding. Breakfast can be ordered all day. They also have great meat-loaf. Healthy alternatives are an option.

Food and Accommodations

Full Moon

344 Huron Avenue
Cambridge, MA 02138
(617) 354-6699

Full Moon

Hours: Mon.-Fri., 11 a.m. - 3 p.m. and 5 p.m. - 9 p.m.; brunch weekends 9 a.m. - 3 p.m. Kids' cooking classes also occasionally offered (with parent in tow).

Directions: This is a driving destination. Call for directions.

This is such a wonderful place, I wish they would open a chain. In my world, every town would have one. Toys, mac-n-cheese, sippy cups if you forgot yours. You are thinking "What's so great about that? I can just stay at home." Well, this restaurant also has gourmet food for the grown-ups. You can have a glass of wine, a delicious salad, and steak, while the kids play nearby. You can probably even finish your dinner without interruption. And the kids love their food too. All kid dishes come with carrot sticks and cut up fruit. The portions are generous and one grown-up friend I go with usually ends up eating part of her daughter's mac-and-cheese; it's that good.

There's a train set up, kitchen, dollhouse, and more. Or, kids can bring a bucket of toys to the table with them. For budding chefs in the family, find out when parent and child cooking classes are held. The cost is $25 per kid (over age 3). Maybe your kids will be making gourmet meals for you someday. A word to the wise: try not to come right at midday. The place is packed, with good reason. If you come around 1 p.m., things are usually a bit calmer, and you don't have to play referee in the toy area with all the children competing for space.

Food and Accommodations

Marche Movenpick

Prudential Center
800 Boylston Street
Boston, MA 02115
(617) 578-9700
www.marcheusa.com

Marche Movenpick

Hours: 7:30 a.m. - 2 a.m.

Directions: Take the Green Line to the Hynes/ICA stop.

Grab your passport and tour the world. Okay, tour the world's food. At Marche Movenpick, you are handed a passport when you enter the restaurant/cafeteria, then you can visit any number of food stations. Whatever you pick will be recorded on your passport, which is then used to tally up the price of your meal. Watch chefs prepare your meal right on the spot. Kids like the freedom and the responsibility of deciding what they want to eat, although don't be surprised if they head straight for the pizza chef, conveniently located right next to the small two-room play area. (It's too bad the play area isn't set up so more tables can see it; adults have to stand nearby to keep an eye on their kids.) You'll probably pay more than you would at the food court on the other side of the mall, but you'll get much better food. Everything looks so tempting, it's easy to load up your tray with more than you'll eat. They also have a food shop downstairs where you can pack a mighty tempting picnic.

Food and Accommodations

North End: anywhere

North End

Directions: Take the Green Line to North Station.

Kids and pasta (not to mention gelato) were made for each other. The one problem with eating in the North End is deciding where to go. Every place tempts you with delicious smells wafting through the doorway. Every pastry shop window seems to have your kids' name written on it. Pizzeria Regina on Thatcher Street is always a good choice. Pitchers of soda, a family atmosphere, and big tables make this Boston restaurant an institution. Hanover Street is the main drag. Dozens of restaurants and bakeries can be found here and on numerous sidestreets.

Redbones

55 Chester Street
Somerville, MA 02144
(617) 628-2200

Redbones

Hours: 11:30 a.m. - 11:30 p.m.

Directions: Take the Red Line to Davis Square.

Note: Cash only.

Messy, loud, and delicious. If you like BBQ—real BBQ, not sauce out of a bottle—go to Redbones. The kids will like all the funky decorations and finger food. You'll like the casual atmosphere. Even vegetarians can make a meal here out of corn fritters, rice and beans, and delicious cornbread. Drinks come in big mugs, and the waitstaff is always friendly. You may have to wait for a table, and don't forget, cash only. (If you do forget anyway, an ATM is just down the street. We've had to run down there more than once.)

Food and Accommodations

Quincy Market

Congress Street
Boston, MA 02109
(617) 338-2323

Quincy Market

Directions: Take the Green Line to Government Center.
Traverse the City Hall Plaza, then cross the street.

I have to include one more major tourist spot because it's convenient, and if you are on the Freedom Trail, it's easy. It's also a good stop if nobody can agree on where to go for dinner. Quincy Market has more than 40 food stalls and plenty of restaurants. Take your pick from pizza, hot dogs, stuffed potatoes, clam chowder, and more. You can eat at little café tables, find a sit-down restaurant, or grab a stroller (sandwich) and head outside if it's nice. I'm sure your kids will point out all the places to get sweets.

Tremont 647

647 Tremont Avenue
Boston, MA 02116
(617) 266-4600

Tremont 647

Pajama Brunch Sundays. 10:30 a.m. - 3 p.m.

On Sunday mornings, the staff wears pajamas and encourages the patrons to do so too. This is a fun way to start off Sunday. Roll out of bed and go get breakfast. You may feel a little silly, but believe me, you get over it fast, and the kids love it. It's very popular, so get there early or be prepared to wait. At least you'll be comfortable. The menu is á la carte. The upscale restaurant is probably not a good spot for children except for the Sunday brunch.

Food and Accommodations

Union Oyster House

Government Center & the North End/Faneuil Hall
41 Union Street
Boston, MA 02108
(617) 227-2750
www.unionoysterhouse.com

Union Oyster House

Hours: Sun.-Thurs, 11 a.m. - 9:30 p.m.; Fri. & Sat. 11 a.m. - 10 p.m. Reservations recommended.

Directions: Take the Blue or Green Line to Government Center. Cross Congress Street. You'll see the sign for the restaurant. On the Freedom Trail, one block from Faneuil Hall.

I certainly can't neglect America's oldest restaurant. The Union Oyster House was established in 1826. It's also near the Faneuil Hall area, making it an easy tourist stop. Don't let the obviousness of the attraction scare you away. It's a pretty neat place, and if your kids won't eat oysters, don't worry, there's plenty else to choose from on the kid's menu. Hamburgers, spaghetti, and grilled cheese, children's staples, are all available. You must get a side order of Boston Baked Beans—they are delicious.

Food and Accommodations

Five Spots to Stay with Kids

Okay, the following hotel rates may not be everybody's idea of cheap, but look closely. Most of them offer a bunch of free things. The complimentary tickets, meals, and parking offered can end up saving you a lot of money. Sit down. Figure out what you want to do and add up all the individual costs. You might be surprised at the total. And, if you're a townie, don't ignore this section. Kids love hotels. They have neat little bars of soap and the ice machines are always lots of fun. Maybe everyone could use a night away from home, even if it is just across town. A new perspective on your city can be gained when you leave the mundane everyday world behind for the weekend.

Something to keep in mind is that most hotels let kids under 12 stay free in the parent's room. Some offer a second, connected room, at half-price for families. Make sure you ask for any family specials at the time. One place to check on the Internet before you book anywhere is the tourist board's website, **www.bostonusa.com**. Click on the family-friendly values section to see what's available. Rates listed below obviously can change, depending on the season and availability.

Food and Accommodations

Best Western Boston

342 Longwood Avenue
Boston, MA 0215
(800) GOT-BEST; (617) 731-4700
www.bestwestern.com

The family package at this conveniently located hotel (it's near the T and the Museum of Fine Arts and Fenway Park) includes a "Kids Love Boston" activity book and either a free movie or an hour of Nintendo in your room. You'll also get 10% off the regular room rate, which starts at $125. Rooms with kitchenettes are also an option for those who want to save on going out to eat.

Boston Harbor Hotel

70 Rowes Wharf
Boston, MA 02110
(800) 752-7077
www.bhh.com

I thought I'd throw in one top-of-the-line package, so I'll tell you right away this "deal" starts at $350. You can't beat the views though. The Boston Harbor Hotel is right on Rowes Wharf. You can walk to Faneuil Hall, the Freedom Trail, and the Aquarium.

The Family Getaway Vacation Package includes accommodations for two adults and two children, breakfast for four in your room or in the restaurant, coloring books and crayons, four tickets to the New England Aquarium, free valet parking, and use of the heath club. In addition, you have the use of cribs, strollers, and games, which can all be brought to the room. The Boston Harbor Hotel also has babysitting available for an additional cost.

Food and Accommodations

The Colonnade

120 Huntington Avenue
Boston, MA 02116
(617) 424-7000; (800) 962-3030
www.colonnadehotel.com

A great location, fabulous restaurant (Brasserie Jo), and interesting packages make this a fun choice. In the summer, there's the only city-view rooftop pool in Boston. Go to the French bistro and tell the kids to order pommes frites. They might be surprised at what they get.

The "Kids See & Do" weekend package includes a one-night stay in a deluxe guestroom, four passes (2 adults/2 children) to the New England Aquarium or the Children's Museum, full American breakfast at Brasserie Jo (in the hotel), overnight parking, and late checkout (2 p.m.). It's $195 per night.

In the winter, the Colonnade has a very clever weekend package called "Frosty Fridays." On Fridays, between November 23 and March 29, you pay whatever the temperature is outside. This could mean you pay just $10 if it's 10 degrees at 5 p.m., when the official temperature for the night is taken.

And, if it's not that cold, you still get a bargain. I mean, you know it's not going to be 80 degrees in Boston in the winter! However, there is a catch: your required Saturday night stay is $239. The package also includes ice-skate rentals and tickets for the Boston Common Frog Pond for two or tickets for the Old Town Trolley, plus French hot cocoa for two at Brasseie Jo and overnight parking. Although this package includes freebies just for two, you'll obviously pay less for children's tickets than you would for the adults, so it's still a good deal for a family.

Food and Accommodations

Hyatt Regency Cambridge

575 Memorial Drive
Cambridge, MA 02139
(800) 233-1234
www.cambridge.hyatt.com

Get a second kid's room for half-price with the "Camp Hyatt" special deal. The kids get a Camp Hyatt hat and passport, an activity book and crayons. Kid's menu and the Disney Channel are available in the room also. The view over the Charles River is beautiful. There is a scheduled shuttle to Boston so the Cambridge location isn't inconvenient for tourists. An indoor pool is another bonus.

Le Meridien

250 Franklin Street
Boston, MA 02110
(800) 791-7762
www.lemeridienboston.com

Who can say no to milk and cookies? The "Voila Splash Package," at $199 per room, includes unlimited Le Club pool privileges, complimentary use of fun floats, special children's welcome basket, and an in-room children's movie. The kids eat free in the Café Fleuri (when accompanied by a parent), you receive savings certificates to local attractions and, finally, there's a nighttime treat of milk and cookies. Kids will adore getting the key to a treasure chest and picking out a toy to keep. If you're feeling flush or have more kids than will fit in your bed, an additional room for children costs $99. Extra nights are $159. Special children's hours at the indoor pool guarantee them free rein of the pool, including toys to play with.

Food and Accommodations

If you're here for Sunday brunch, check out the "Kid's Corner" in Café Fleuri. It is kid-food heaven, with mini-pizzas, hot dogs, tacos, chicken fingers and macaroni and cheese, plus popcorn, potato chips, fruit kabobs, cookies, and brownies. There are six other brunch stations if you'd rather have crepes than mac-n-cheese. Price for brunch is $42 for adults; $19 for children under 12; and children under 4 are free.

Midtown Hotel

220 Huntington Avenue
Boston, MA 02115
(800) 343-1177; (617) 262-1000
www.midtownhotel.com

The Midtown rates start at $99 and its location can't be beat, right on Huntington Avenue near the Prudential Building, Copley Square, and many other attractions. Although, even without any special deals, the Midtown is a bargain for the city, many specials are offered throughout the year, making it even more attractive. The winter family value package gives an additional 15% off the price of a room plus free parking. Theme deals include hotel stay and tickets to a show in town or passes to a museum. A recent look at the website showed a "Boston Cook's" package, which included the room and a roundtrip taxi voucher to any restaurant in town. The "Holiday Shopper's Special" deal included free gift-wrapping! Now, if they threw in babysitting...

6 | Day Trips

If you never left Boston's city limits, you'd have enough to keep you busy for years, but there are many important and interesting sites nearby. If you want to see where the Puritans first landed, you'll have to go south to Plymouth. Concord and Lexington, with the North Bridge and the Lexington Green, also set the stage for the American Revolution. Salem, or "Witch City," is a big lure year-round, not just at Halloween, and besides fascinating the children with its grisly past, the town is a wonderful place to explore. You have to leave Boston and head west if you want to get lost in a giant maze in a corn field or to visit the first polar bear born in New England.

Day trips usually mean car trips, but some places are easy to get to by train. My usual criterion for a day trip is that it has to be less than a two-hour drive each way. Most of these sights are actually less than an hour, making them more of a morning or afternoon trip, but I have included a few that are longer because they shouldn't be missed.

Day Trips

North

Concord & Lexington

If you are doing the history thing with your kids, you'll definitely want to head up north to Concord and Lexington for the other part of the story. While many exciting events occurred in Boston, you have to go to Lexington and Concord to see the North Bridge, where "the shot heard 'round the world" was fired and the Lexington Battle Green. In addition to all the history you'll absorb, both towns are beautiful and full of quaint shops and restaurants. Walking around in the fall is particularly spectacular.

There are visitor's centers both in Lexington and Concord that can help you with maps and other information. Special tours and re-enactments are common.

Lexington Visitor's Center

(781) 862-1450
www.lexingtonchamber.org

Concord Visitor's Center

(978) 369-3120
www.lexington-concord.org

Day Trips

Concord

Concord Museum

**Concord Museum
200 Lexington Road (Entrance on Cambridge Tpke.)
Concord, MA 01742
(978) 369-9763
www.concordmuseum.org**

Concord Museum

Hours: Jan.-Mar., Mon.-Sat., 11 a.m. - 4 p.m.; Sun., 1-4 p.m.; Apr.-Dec., Mon.-Sat., 9 a.m. - 5 p.m.; Sun., noon-5 p.m.

Admission: adults, $7; children 6-17, $3; family pass, good for two adults & 4 kids, $16. There's a discount for AAA members.

Directions: Take 95 North to Route 2 West (Exit 30B). Take Route 2A toward Concord Center. When road splits into a V, head right toward Concord Center.

The Concord Museum was established in 1886 and is full of artifacts dating back to the 17th century. The lantern that hung in the Old North Church the night of Paul Revere's ride is here as well as items from the American Revolution. The "Why Concord?" exhibit is very informative and details Concord's place in history. Your kids might not be thrilled that the museum has the "world's largest collection of Thoreau possessions," but there are other things to interest them. Pick up an activity pack when you come in to help you explore. The backpack includes reproduced artifacts such as a spy glass, quill, and slate (and much more) and a trail guide. This has directions, a treasure hunt and fun games related to exhibits. Kids eat this stuff up.

The "Artifacts of Childhood" exhibit should also grab kids' attention, showing a glimpse rarely seen into earlier eras of childhood. A children's story hour is held every fourth Friday of the month October-May for kids ages 3-5 at 1 p.m. Not only is there a story, but also a snack and a hands-on activity. The cost is $7 per child (adult, free). Sundays are sometimes "Family Sampler Sundays" with tours and activities. For Massachusetts residents, the "Be Our Guest" program during the winter offers free museum admission for various communities. Check for dates.

Day Trips

Minute Man National Historical Park/ North Bridge

Minute Man Visitor Center
174 Liberty Street
Concord, MA 01742
(978) 369-6993
www.nps.gov/mima

Minute Man National Historical Park/ North Bridge

Hours: daily, 9 a.m. - 5 p.m.

Directions: Take I-93 North to Exit 30.

The North Bridge, of course, is where "the shot heard 'round the world" was fired. You can walk over the bridge and see the "Minute Man Statue" commemorating the events that famous day of April 19, 1775. Start off at the visitor's center for a theater program and brochures. Only the most active or ambitious families will follow the 5.5-mile-long Battle Road Trail, but even walking part of it is a lovely stroll.

Orchard House

399 Lexington Road
Concord, MA 01742
(978) 369-4118
www.louisamayalcott.org

If you are familiar with *Little Women*, you may want to visit the house where it is believed author Louisa May Alcott set the book. If you take the Literary Trail tour, you'll come by on your tour. The house is much like it was when the Alcotts lived here, from 1858-1877.

Orchard House usually has a few special events a month, many geared towards families. The "Hand-in-Hand at Orchard House" is an example of a program for children under six with a parent. A tour, dressing up in Victorian clothes, games, and songs are all part of the fun.

Orchard House

Hours: Apr.-Oct., 10 a.m. - 4:30 p.m. & Sun. 1-4 p.m.; Nov.-Mar., Mon.-Fri., 11 a.m. - 3 p.m.; Sat., 10 a.m. - 4:30 p.m.; Sun., 1-4:30 p.m. Tours are guided only and given on the half-hour. Call ahead; they sell out when they have groups.

Admission: adults, $7; children, 6-17, $4; family rate (2 adults, 4 kids, $16).

Directions: Take 95 North to Route 2 West (Exit 30B). Take Route 2A toward Concord Center. When road splits into a V, head right toward Concord Center. It's 2.5 miles on the right.

Day Trips

Old Manse

269 Monument Street
Concord, MA 01742
(978) 369-3909

Old Manse

Hours: mid-Apr. to Oct., Mon.-Sat., 10 a.m. - 5 p.m.; Sun. and holidays, noon - 5 p.m.

Directions: Take I-93 North to Exit 30. Follow signs.

The Old Manse, home to Ralph Waldo Emerson, was built by his grandfather William Emerson in 1770. The North Bridge, which is nearby, is visible from the upstairs rooms. The elder Emerson wrote about the famous events that occurred in the region. Many years later his grandson wrote *Nature* here. Later, Nathaniel Hawthorne and his wife lived here as well, and were very happy. You can see where they scratched their names and little messages to each other in windowpanes throughout the house. This is one of the stops on the Literary Trail Tour (see Chapter Three). If you are going to visit the North Bridge anyway, stop in.

Day Trips

Walden Pond State Reservation

915 Walden Street
Concord, MA 01742
(978) 369-3254
www.state.ma.us/dem/parks/wldn.htm

Walden Pond State Reservation

Hours: dawn to dusk.

Admission: $5 per car.

Directions: From Boston: take Route 2 West to Route 126 South. Follow signs.

This is one of my absolute favorite day trips. And I'm not the only one who counts this as a great destination, especially in the summer; if you get here too late, you're out of luck. When the parking lot fills up, no one else is allowed in. So get here early, bring a lunch and an umbrella, and prepare to relax. Swimming in Henry David Thoreau's former backyard is a joy for parents and their children. Lifeguards patrol a roped-off area on a small beach where most families park themselves. The shallow water extends for several feet and allows little ones to splash around in safety. You can swim beyond the ropes if you want, but they make a good boundary for the children. If you want to get out of the water, take a walk around the pond.

A bathhouse makes changing clothes convenient. About the only food around is an ice-cream truck usually parked in the parking lot, so be sure to bring food and water if you'll be here for a while. Although the pond has a lot of shade, it's all far away from the beach area. Bring an umbrella. Occasionally the park rangers host activities for children. After one visit, my daughter brought home a sun catcher she made with an old CD and beads. If you get tired of swimming or you're a big Thoreau fan, visit the replica of Thoreau's cabin. It's by the parking lot. Rangers give talks in the summer.

Day Trips

Lexington

Lexington Battle Green

Bedford & Massachusetts Avenue
Lexington, MA 02401
(781) 862-1450

Lexington Battle Green

Directions: Take Route 93 North to Route 95 South to exit 31A (Rts. 4 & 225, Lexington). Take a right off exit onto Bedford St. Go through 3 traffic lights and Bedford St. runs into Massachusetts Avenue.

You might want to start off at the Chamber of Commerce Visitor's Center where there is a diorama of the battle and all sorts of information on where the first skirmish of the American Revolution occurred. (Don't be confused by all the firsts everywhere. There are different shades of meaning to them all.) On the Green, there's a statue of Captain Parker and the Revolutionary Monument. You can also see the Old Belfry that alerted the militia.

Museum of Our National Heritage

33 Marrett Road/Route 2A
Lexington, MA 02401
(781) 861-6559
www.monh.org

Museum of Our National Heritage

Directions: Take Route 128 to Exit 30A (2A East, also known as Marrett Road). The Museum is 3 miles on the left with a brick entrance and large iron gates.

To get a more detailed look at what happened in Lexington, you should visit the Museum of Our National Heritage. The permanent exhibit "Lexington Alarm'd" is filled with everything you'd ever wanted to know about that fateful day. Hands-on exhibits should interest the kids. The museum doesn't limit itself to just this one event. There are many other permanent and special exhibits focusing on everything from clocks to items made in Massachusetts.

Family programs are very hands-on and lots of fun for kids. One recent family day was tied into an exhibit on milk delivery in New England (don't laugh, it was really neat!). We churned butter, made milk paint and a cow puppet. It was just $5 for the family. Other programs like children's workshops and lectures are offered.

Day Trips

Salem

Salem

Directions: Located 16 miles north of Boston. It's easy to drive or take the train to Salem. Once there, you don't need a car. It's a very walkable city.

By car: take Route 128 North to exit 25A and follow Route 114 East into Salem. Follow signs to the Salem Visitor Center, Museum and Historic Sites, and Downtown parking.

By train: take the MBTA Newburyport/Rockport commuter rail train from North Station to the Salem depot. It's a five-minute walk to the Visitor Center (59 Wharf St; 877-SALEMMA).

Salem is an eclectic mix of true historical sites (such as the House of Seven Gables), cheesy museums (the Museum of Myths & Monsters), and modern-day witches (who proudly proclaim their wiccan colors). It's fun to explore this waterfront town, with its neat giftshops and seafood restaurants.

I've listed a few places you shouldn't miss if you are visiting Salem. Wandering around on your own, you'll find a lot more to experience. Salem has its own heritage trail to follow, just like Boston, and it is painted red too. Stop in at the Visitor Center for a map.

Salem Witch Museum

Washington Square
Salem, MA 01970
879-744-1692
www.salemwitchmuseum.com

Salem Witch Museum

Hours: 10 a.m. - 5 p.m., daily. Open until 7 p.m. in July and August.

Admission: adult, $6; children, $4.

Directions: The museum is diagonally across from the Common in downtown Salem. Directions to Salem are above in Salem entry.

The museum is a mini-education about the witch hysteria of 1692. Thirteen (yes, unlucky 13) stage sets display the story of what really happened in Salem when 19 hapless souls lost their lives to the hysteria of the times. The somewhat cheesy presentation might at times be scary for the little ones. Another exhibit, called "Witches, Evolving Perceptions," will set you and your kids straight on the truth about witches and their religion.

Day Trips

The House of the Seven Gables Historic Site

54 Turner Street
Salem, MA 01970
(978) 744-0991
www.7gables.org

The House of the Seven Gables Historic Site also includes Nathaniel Hawthorne's Birthplace, the Retire Beckett House, the Hooper-Hathaway House, and a Counting House. Your admission allows you to roam around them all. The kids all love the secret staircase in the House of the Seven Gables, which was used to hide supposed witches, and later, runaway slaves. You can combine this visit with one to the living history museum, Salem 1630: Pioneer Village and get a sense of what life was like in the 17th century.

> **The House of the Seven Gables Historic Site**
>
> Hours: late Jan. to mid-Apr., Mon.-Sat., 10 a.m. - 5 p.m. and Sun., noon - 5 p.m. Open later July-Oct., until 7 p.m.; Nov. & Dec., 10 a.m. - 5 p.m. Closed the first three weeks of January.
>
> Admission: adults, $8; children, 6-17, $6; under 6, free.
>
> Directions: Take I-95 North (Route 128) to Exit 25A to Route 114. Follow Route 114 East to Salem Center. Follow the "Waterfront" signs to Derby Street. Visitor maps and signs posted throughout the city point the way.

Day Trips

Parlee Farms

Farwell Road
Tyngsboro, MA 01879
(978) 649-3854
www.parleefarm.com

Parlee Farms makes a delightful family outing, with something for everyone: a variety of fruits and flowers for picking, a clean and well-arranged farm animal petting zoo, a fun Hay Play Area, a demonstration beehive, and an attractive farm stand. Three generations of my family were thrilled to find plentiful raspberries and strawberries, as well as autumnal apples and pumpkins, on a mid-September afternoon. The farm uses ladybugs, rather than pesticides to control insects, so you can let the kids snack in the fields without worrying about harmful poisons. This is a better fall excursion, rather than summer, since heat makes picking a lot less fun. However, during the summer season a free hayride takes you from one field to the next, which kids always like (what is it about hay, anyway?).

Parlee Farms

June hours: daily 7 a.m. - 6 p.m.; July 4th, 7 a.m. - 1 p.m.

Summer hours: (July 5-Sept. 2) Tues.-Sat, 8 a.m. - 6 p.m.; Sun., 8 a.m. - 3 p.m.; closed Mon.

Fall hours: (Sept. 3-Oct. 21) Tues.-Sun, 10 a.m. - 5 p.m.; closed Mondays except Labor Day and Columbus Day.

Directions: Take Route 3 north to Exit 34, Westford Rd. in Tyngsboro. Go right onto Westford Rd. and continue one mile to lights, then go left onto Middlesex Rd. Take second right onto Farwell Rd. (just after Tyngsboro Bridge). Farm is one mile down on the right.

Day Trips

Stone Zoo

149 Pond Street
Stoneham, MA 02180
(781) 438-5100
www.zoonewengland.com

The Stone Zoo, sister to Boston's Franklin Park Zoo, doesn't have as much to offer as a zoo, but there is an annual event here not to be missed. It's called Zoolights and is held every December. Thousands and thousands of lights make a magical land between 5-9 p.m. Santa is on hand to greet visitors (and pose for photos). You'll head down Snowy Owl Creek trail and be enchanted by all the animals, real and fake. Every year it seems the zoo adds new features. The latest attraction is a carousel and kiddie rides. (Admission to Zoolights is $3; under 2, free.)

If you're not here for the lights, you must be here for the animals. There's a barnyard area for petting goats and sheep. The "Snowy Owl Creek" exhibit allows you to view animals not found at many other zoos. Look for snowy owls, lynx, artic foxes, and reindeer. After construction is completed in the spring of 2002, a new exhibit, "Treasures of the Sierra Madre," should be a crowd-pleaser, with jaguars, cougars, Gila monsters, bats, and other animals found in American Southwest and Mexico.

Stone Zoo

Hours: Apr.-Sept., 10 a.m. - 5 p.m. (weekends and holidays until 6 p.m.); Oct.-Mar., daily 10 a.m. - 4 p.m.

Admission: adults, $6, children 2-15, $4; under 2, free.

Directions: From Boston, take I-93 North to Exit 35. Turn left at the bottom of the ramp and follow the signs.

Day Trips

Wolf Hollow

144 Essex Road, Route 133
Ipswich, MA 01938
(978) 356-0216

For one of the most unusual animal encounters you can get, go to Wolf Hollow and see the endangered gray wolf. The nonprofit North American Wolf Foundation was started by husband-and-wife team Paul and Joni Soffron pretty much in their back yard. Its mission is to educate the public about how gray wolves benefit our environment. Viewing the behavior of the pack of wolves is amazing. The wolves consider the couple as part of their pack. The weekend programs, consisting of a lecture and demonstration, last an hour, and you'll be riveted the whole time, although you might be a little uncomfortable on the wooden benches.

Wolf Hollow

Hours: Saturday & Sunday at 1:30 p.m. & 3:30 p.m.

Admission: adults, $4.50; children 3-17, $3.

Directions: From Boston, take 128 North to Exit 14, 133 West to Ipswich.

Day Trips

West

The Butterfly Place

120 Tyngsboro Road
Westford, MA 01886
(978) 392-0955
www.butterflyplace-ma.com

The Butterfly Place

Hours: Mar. 1-Columbus Day 10 a.m. - 5 p.m.

Admission: adults, $7.50; children, 3-12, $5.50; under 3, free.

Directions: Take the Mass Turnpike to 128 North. Get on Route 3 North and get off at Exit 34. Take Westford Road to Swan Road, which becomes Tyngsboro Road. Go 1 mile and it's on the right.

Clearly, this is another destination with one thing as its specialty. The Butterfly Place, with its 27-foot atrium holding as many as 500 butterflies at once, is both interesting and beautiful—if you're into butterflies. Don't bring kids here thinking they'll immediately be transfixed. Children under three have to be in a stroller, backpack, or held by the hand at all times. An introductory video, display cases, and observation room supplement the atrium. Pick up a Papillon Hatching Kit in the gift shop and let the kids watch their own caterpillar turn into a butterfly at home.

Bob Wilson

Check out the beautiful flutterby, I mean butterfly.

Day Trips

Davis' Farmland & Mega Maze

Redstone Hill
Sterling, MA 01564
(978) 422-MOOO; (978) 422-8888
www.davisfarmland.com; www.davismegamaze.com

This place is so much fun that you'll forgive the hour-plus it takes to get here. If you have a mixed-age group, you can always visit both the Farmland and the Mega Maze, but plan on a full day to do both. The complex is run by seventh-generation Davis' family members. When farming wasn't making money for them anymore, they turned the land into a more profitable venture. Lucky for us they did.

The Farmland is brilliantly designed so that you can see your child wherever they are by standing in the middle of the grounds. This allows you to let your kids roam free, as the animals do. The Farmland is the perfect size for a grand younger kid adventure. They say they cater to the under-eight set here, but I'm guessing older kids will like the animals too. Children are encouraged to go right into most of the animal pens if they like. We spent a good half-hour watching as our daughter hugged all the little kids (goats, that is) she could find. The goat-milking demonstration was also a huge hit. The Farm is more than a mere petting zoo though. It is home to many rare endangered species of livestock, which the Davis' are trying to breed to save them from extinction. There is a concession stand and picnic area.

The Mega Maze is definitely aimed at adults and older kids. It's an amazing example of what you can do with a tractor and a cornfield. Each year a master maze maker from England redesigns the maze and it takes on a new theme. One year it was in the shape of a UFO. The following year it was a T-Rex. There are always several ways to solve the maze, but don't worry if you can't.

Jennifer Bester

Kid brushing kid at Davis Farmland.

Day Trips

Davis' Farmland & Mega Maze

Farmland: open weather permitting,
April 12-Sept. 3, daily 9:30 a.m. - 4:30 p.m.; Sept. 6-October, Thurs.-Sun., same hours.

Mega Maze: weather permitting, mid-July through Sept. 3, daily 10 a.m. - 5 p.m.; Sept.-Oct., weekends only.

Admission: Farmland – general admission, $8.95; under 2, free. Mega Maze – adults, $9.95; kids under 14, $7.95; under 4, free. Combo pass to both: adults, $16.40; under 14, $14.40. (These are weekend prices; it's a dollar cheaper on weekdays.)

Directions: One hour from Boston. Take I-90 West (Mass Pike) to Exit 26, then Route 62 West (9.3 miles) and follow the signs. The Farmland and Mega Maze are across the road from each other.

There are friendly maze guides on patrol to point you in the right direction (and they never lie). If you are positive that you'll get lost, you can carry a flag and wave it for help. Make sure your kids are up for the challenge. It can be a little claustrophobic and being stuck in a cornfield with a screaming toddler is no fun. Stick to the Farmland if you think that might be a problem.

DeCordova Museum and Sculpture Park

51 Sandy Pond Road
Lincoln, MA 01773
(781) 259-8355
www.decordova.org

DeCordova Museum and Sculpture Park

Hours: Tues.-Sun., 11 a.m. - 5 p.m. Sculpture Park open daily.

Admission: adults, $6; children 5 and under, free.

Directions: From Boston, take Route 128 North/I-95 North to Exit 28, Trapelo Road/Lincoln. Follow Trapelo Road 2.5 miles to stop sign. Continue straight onto Sandy Pond Road. The museum is 1/2 mile on the right.

The DeCordova Museum & Sculpture Park is great fun, especially for kids who get itchy in museums. Examining the more than 70 outdoor sculptures is definitely an adventure for the kids, and they'll like the fact that no one is warning them not to touch. They are even encouraged to pick up sticks from the grounds and play on a giant xylophone. An added bonus is that the DeCordova is set on 35 acres in scenic Lincoln. Bring a picnic in nice weather. Modern and contemporary art are the focus of the museum, which was formerly the estate of Julian de Cordova. The annual hands-on Art in the Park festival every summer is a big draw.

Annual Art in the Park festival.

Day Trips

Discovery Museums

177 Main Street
Acton, MA 01720
(978) 264-4201
www.ultranet.com/~discover

Discovery Museums

Sept.-Jun.: Children's Museum open Tues. & Fri., 1-4:30 p.m.; Wed. & Thurs., 9 a.m. - 4:30 p.m. Science Museum open Tues., Thurs. & Fri. 1-4:30 p.m.; Wed., 1-6 p.m. Both open on weekends 9 a.m. - 4:30 p.m.

Summer: Both museums open Tues.-Sun., 9 a.m. - 4:30 p.m.

Admission: $7 for one museum; $10 for both.

Directions: From Boston, take Route 128 North to Route 2 West. Go around the Concord rotary, stay on Route 2 another 2 miles. Take Route 27 South toward Maynard. Museums 1 mile on left.

This duo is a sure-fire winner for residents tired of the city and looking for something different to do. As a tourist, you probably wouldn't want to make a special trip. Visitors to one museum will definitely want to go to the other, so buy the $10 ticket up front. The Children's Museum is pretty small and only limited numbers of people are allowed in at one time. I love this policy. There's never a chance of the overcrowding which is often an issue at other museums. If you can't get in right away, there's always room at the much bigger Science Museum next door. The Children's Museum is like a giant doll's house, or the house your kids would design if you'd let them. Each room explores a different theme. There's the Train Room, Bessie's Play Diner, Woodland Room, and several others. You get the picture. This is definitely designed for younger children.

The Science Museum is geared toward older children, but my preschooler and her friend enjoyed it too. They wanted to get their little hands on the tools in the Inventor's Workshop (you have to be six for that exhibit). Instead, they contented themselves with percussion instruments in the Music Room.

My major complaint about the Discovery Museums is that there is no lunchroom area. There are picnic tables outside, but these work only in nice weather. So if you are here during lunchtime, you either have to sneak your lunch in a staircase like we did, eat in the car, or head home.

Day Trips

Drumlin Farm Wildlife Sanctuary

South Great Road, Route 117
Lincoln, MA 01773
(617) 259-9807
www.massaudubon.org

Drumlin Farm
Wildlife Sanctuary

Hours: Mar.-Oct., Tues.-Sun. 9 a.m. - 5 p.m. and Monday holidays; Nov.-Feb., closes at 4 p.m.

Admission: adults, $6; children 3-12, $4 (free to Mass Audubon Society members).

Directions: From Boston, take I-90 West to Rt. 128 North. Left on Rt. 117. Go about 5 miles.

   The Massachusetts Audubon Society runs this 250-acre working farm which is home to pigs, cows, horses, the works. The ubiquitous hayride is available for $1. In addition to the old favorites, there is the Burrowing Animal Building, with foxes and woodchucks; trails to explore; and gardens to poke around in. A gift shop and small farm stand are located near the entrance.

   Myriad programs and demonstrations are held throughout the year. Examples include helping the farmers in the "See How it Grew" program, where kids and their parents help put the farm's garden to rest in the winter. In the fun "Farmers" Helper" program kids help with milking, collecting eggs and other farmyard chores. There are eight-week programs, but many one-day lectures and other events may coincide with a visit.

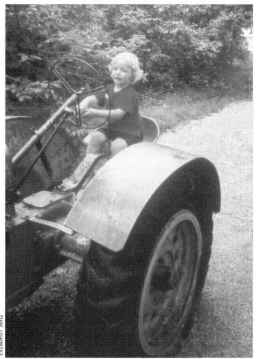

Ready to plow at Drumlin Farm.

Elizabeth Seitz

141

Day Trips

Ecotarium

222 Harrington Way
Worcester, MA 01604
(508) 929-2700
www.ecotarium.org

Many people have problems with zoos, with animals used as displays to entertain. If you feel that way, but still like to see wild creatures up close, this is the place for you. The Ecotarium has a raise-and-release program and houses animals that can't live in the wild for whatever reason. Some have been injured or are ill, others have had too much contact with humans to make it alone in the wild. Kendra the polar bear is a huge draw, as she was born here in 1984 and is the first polar bear born in New England to survive. Annually, red-bellied turtles spend winter at the Ecotarium and then are released in spring. Permanent residents include bald eagles, otters, and bobcats.

Ecotarium

Hours: Tues.-Sat.,10 am-5 pm; Sun., noon-5 pm. Open Monday holidays.

Admission: Adults, $7; children, 3-16, $5; under 3, free. Express train tickets, $2. On the first Sunday of every month, admission is free from 2-5 pm.

Directions: From Boston, take the Mass Pike West to Exit 11. Take a left on Route 122 North. Go 3 miles and take a right on Plantation Street. Go 1 mile to Franklin Street and take a right. Take the second right onto Harrington Way. The Ecotarium is past the baseball field on the left. It will take a little over an hour to get here.

The Explorer Express Train (additional $2) takes visitors through the grounds in a mini-copy of an 1860s steam-engine train. The Preschool Room is stocked with activities, books, and ferrets and makes a nice stop for those with children under 5. Children can look through giant microscopes or listen to animal sounds on earphones. The Planetarium ($2.50 admission) offers all sorts of interesting programs, including one that looks into what the stars meant to Native Americans and ancient Greeks.

It may seem that every time you turn around, you're asked to pay another fee, but it's all for a good cause. And truly, this is a unique place. You're not going to find many sites where you can actually explore the treetops. In fact, you won't find any others in this country. The exhibit, for those not afraid of heights, is called the Tree Canopy Walkway (kids must be seven or older, accompanied by an adult). A series of cable walkways suspended 40 feet up is modeled after those in tropical rainforests and allows you to explore a region usually reserved for the birds. Don't worry, you don't have to go it alone. This is an hour-long guided exhibit, and you must register in advance. You'll be harnessed up, complete with helmet, and up you go, eye-level with many creatures you'd never see down below.

Day Trips

Nashoba Valley Winery

100 Wattaquadoc Hill Road
Bolton, MA 01740
(978) 779-5521
www.nashobawinery.com

> **Nashoba Valley Winery**
>
> Open year-round. Call to find out what's in season.
>
> Directions: Take the Mass Pike West to 495 North. Take exit 17 (Route 117 West) and go 1 mile to Bolton Center. Turn left on Wattaquadoc Hill Road (blinking light). The Winery is 1/4 down on the right. It's less than 40 minutes from Boston.

Don't get nervous. I'm not throwing caution to the wind and getting the toddlers tipsy. Nashoba Valley Winery is much more than a winery. At least 100 varieties of apples are grown here, waiting for you to pick them in season, as well as plums, raspberries, strawberries, peaches, and more. All this fruit is used in the different varieties of wines Nashoba produces, but you can have the fruit in its purest form, freshly plucked. And if you get tired before you have enough to take home, you can take the easy way out and do your picking from bushels.

We make an annual pilgrimage in the fall and attend either the Harvest Festival in September or their Oktoberfest. Along with the apple picking, there's music, entertainment, and food. It is such a beautiful setting that it's easy to just hang out all day. Call to get the season's schedules for fruit picking. There's also a store if you want to take home some of the Winery's wares or locally produced condiments and a restaurant open for lunch and dinner.

Day Trips

Old Sturbridge Village

One Old Sturbridge Village Road, Route 20
Sturbridge, MA 01566
(508) 347-3363
www.osv.org

Old Sturbridge Village a living history museum permanently set in the years 1790 to 1840. These museums (Plimouth Plantation, Salem 1630, etc.) can go either way for kids. Either the novelty of people in period costume speaking in dialect is fun and novel, or it's a bore. Sturbridge Village is very large, with more than 40 buildings, plus animals, and lots of hands-on activities. It usually has a lot going on so you're bound to find something to entertain the kids, no matter their age.

When you get your ticket, you'll receive a map and a list of that day's events. After the orientation program, you can plan the rest of your visit. You'll definitely need at least a few hours. The Samson's Children's Museum should be the first stop for those with smaller children. A dress-up area, play kitchen, and schoolroom are all inviting places to play and not a heavy-handed way to learn about the past. In the warmer months, a ride on the Quinebag River is a treat (costs $3; under 3, free).

There are plenty of choices for eating, from a cafeteria to a tavern or a café, or you can bring your own picnic. On the day you visit, you may be able to watch a 19th century magic show or drop in for games at the Town Pound. Periodically,

Old Sturbridge Village

Hours: Apr.-Oct., daily 9 a.m. - 5 p.m.; Nov., daily 10 a.m. - 4 p.m.; Jan. - mid-Feb., weekends, 10 a.m. - 4 p.m.; mid-Feb. - Mar., Tues.-Sun., 10 a.m. - 4 p.m. (Call for specific dates as they change annually.)

Admission: adults, $20; children 6-15, $10; under 6, free. Tickets are good for two consecutive days.

Directions: About an hour from Boston. Take the Mass. Turnpike (I-90) to Exit 9. Follow signs.

there are special dinner events at Sturbridge Village. For example, you can come to Families Cook, an event where you prepare dinner by the hearth with the costumed interpreters assisting you. A calendar of events listed on the website is helpful to look at when planning your visit. For additional fees, there are hands-on activities for children such as making wood toys or learning how to stencil. You don't have to get too hung up on planning unless there is something specific you want to do. There is usually a wide variety of options on any given day. People who live in the area with children ages 8-12 should check out the Kids Club. It costs $10 for a year membership, which allows the child free unlimited admission when accompanied by an adult, a quarterly newsletter, and discounts on activities at the Village.

Launching a toy hot air balloon at Old Sturbridge Village.

Thomas Neill

Day Trips

South

Edaville Railroad

Route 58
South Carver, MA 02366
(508) 866-8190; 877-EDAVILLE
www.edaville.org

Edaville Railroad

Hours: June-Oct., daily 10 a.m. - 5 p.m.; Nov.-Jan., Mon.-Fri., 4-9 p.m., Sat. & Sun. 2-9 p.m.

Admission: Summer/Fall: adults, $12.50; children 3-12, $8.50; under 3, free. Holiday Festival of Lights rates, Nov. 9-Jan. 6: adults, $15; children, $10.

Directions: One hour from Boston. Take Route 3 South to Route 44 West to Route 58 South. Follow for about 7 miles and the railroad is on the left at Rochester Road.

Edaville Railroad takes you on a nostalgic trip back to old-fashioned amusements. Ride the old-timey carousel, watch the smaller children enjoy the kiddie rides, and by all means, jump on board the authentic two-foot narrow-gauge railway. Steam and diesel locomotives pull passenger cars on a 5.5-mile trip through 1,800 acres of cranberry bogs. (Everything is included in the admission price.) A playground area with wooden train cars is fun for the little ones, and you can climb in old train car engines near the railway as well as on an old fire engine.

Jennifer Bester

An old fire engine is part of the charm at Edaville Railroad.

The Christmas Light Festival is a big draw here, when the place gets gussied up as a winter wonderland, but any time is fun. It's definitely worth the drive from Boston if you live here. If you are just visiting for a few days, you might not want to dedicate the time it takes to get here and back.

Day Trips

Plimoth Plantation & the *Mayflower II*

137 Warren Avenue
Plymouth, MA 02360
(508) 746-4978
www.plimoth.org

Plimoth Plantation

Visit the year 1627 in this re-creation of a Pilgrim village (about 20 structures) and Hobbamock's (Wampanoag Indian) Homesite. Trained staff dress and speak as though they were in the 17th century. It amuses some kids, and adults too, to try to trip up the Pilgrims with modern-day questions, but they are too well-trained. They'll give you a puzzled look if you ask what kind of computer they use. This living history museum is a great way to impart an important part of our past. The staff can tell you how they

A bake oven at Plimoth Plantation.

cook on a hearth or how difficult the winters are, all in period dialect. In Hobbamock's Homesite (where interpreters speak modern-day English), you can perhaps watch a canoe being built or visit the wetuash (houses). Hobbanock was a Pokanoket Indian and Plymouth Colony's interpreter and guide. Older children and adults will get more out of this museum than smaller children.

Day Trips

Mayflower II

The *Mayflower II* is part of the museum complex although it is located on the Plymouth waterfront. As you can probably surmise from the ship's name, this is a re-creation of what the original *Mayflower* that brought the pilgrims to New England might have been like. You'll also find costumed interpreters on board more than willing to tell you how hard sailing over the ocean was in 1620. There are exhibits placed right outside the ship explaining why the Pilgrims left England, which native people they encountered on arrival, and navigation techniques. The kids can have fun playing games their 17th century counterparts played, such as bubbles.

Plymouth Rock

Plymouth Waterfront

A hop, skip and a jump from the *Mayflower II* is that most-famous rock, Plymouth Rock. Supposedly, the Pilgrims used the stone when stepping out of their ship. It's hard not to be disappointed when you see it; after all, it's just a rock. Try to remember its symbolic meaning as the place where the Pilgrims first landed.

The *Mayflower II* docked in Plymouth.

Ted Curtin for Plimoth Plantation

Plimoth Plantation & the *Mayflower II*

Hours: daily 9 a.m. –5 p.m.

Admission: combo pass (good for two days) for Plimoth Plantation & Mayflower II: adult, $22; child, $14. Plantation-only ticket: adult, $20; child, $12. Mayflower II only: adult, $8; child, $6. Under 5, free.

Directions: Located one hour south of Boston. Take Route 3 South to Exit 4. Follow the signs to Plimoth Plantation. The Mayflower II is on the Plymouth waterfront, 3 miles from Plimoth Plantation at State Pier.

Day Trips

Southwick's Zoo

2 Southwick Street
Mendon, MA 01756
(508) 883-9182
www.southwickszoo.com

Southwick's Zoo

Hours: May-Oct., 10 a.m. - 5 p.m.

Admission: adults, $13.50; children 3-12, $9.50.

Directions: From Boston, take Mass Pike West to 495 South to Exit 20. Take Route 85 South to Route 16 West. Follow Route 16 into Mendon and turn right at the Texaco. Follow the signs.

Why should I drive an hour and pay an arm and a leg to go to a zoo, you ask? Well, the sheer size of this zoo and the number of animals it has makes it the largest zoo in New England. Prices are a little steep because it's privately owned. Like Davis Farmland, the Southwick's Zoo was once a real working farm.

Prepare to spend all day here because that's the only way you'll even see half of the animals on the 300-acre zoo. You'll probably get caught up attending presentations and shows offered throughout the day. The 35-acre deer forest is a great exhibit. You can buy feed, stroll through the forest, and the deer will come eat right out of your hand! Southwick's Zoo is also more than just a showcase for animals. Earth Limited operates from the zoo, educating the public about environmentalism and animal ecology. A petting zoo, rides, and playground made completely out of recycled materials will certainly call to your kids.

Day Trips

World's End

250 Martins Lane
Hingham, MA 02043
(781) 821-2977
www.thetrustees.org

World's End

Hours: mid-Apr. to mid-Sept., 8 a.m. - 8 p.m.; the rest of the year the park closes at 5 p.m.

Admission: adults, $4.50; under 12, free.

Directions: From Boston, take Route 3 to Exit 14. Follow 228 North toward Hingham for 6.5 miles. Turn left on Route 3A. Turn right on Summer Street. Continue straight until the end (name changes to Martin's Lane).

You might be surprised to see Frederick Law Olmsted's name popping up here, but yes, he did have a plan for this section of Hingham. In the 19th century, John Brewer, who owned the land, wanted to parcel it in house plots and hired Olmsted to design the grounds. Luckily for us, only the good remains, as the development never happened. The Trustees for Preservation bought the land and set it aside for public use. Olmsted's paths and walkways remain, but there are no houses to spoil the view. Hiking and walking are the main activities on the 200-plus-acre peninsula. Archaeologists think that the site was a seasonal campsite for Native Americans. We go there seasonally, too. In warm weather, it's a great place to just kick back and have a picnic. This is no place for a stroller, though. Bring a kiddie backpack for the small ones.

The Trustees also have a variety of programs at World's End that should interest children. Say you have an early riser in the family. You might enjoy an informal bird walk on a Saturday morning at 7 a.m. ($4; kids under 12 free). Or maybe your kid has the makings of an animal tracker (just don't ask him to find his lost shoe). On snow days, he or she can learn what animals are busy in the winter and what their tracks look like ($4.50; under 12, free). Call about the many other events scheduled throughout the year.

7 Suggested Itineraries & Tours

The first two tours here are targeted more for the infrequent visitor unfamiliar with the city, although those bored with their regular routines might get inspired. The Island Getaways section offers detailed information on taking a trip down to Martha's Vineyard or Nantucket, two places everyone ought to visit at least once in their lives.

Chapter Seven

Whirlwind Weekend Tour

No matter the season, start your first day off at the Boston Common. If it's summer, you can splash around in the **Frog Pond** after sightseeing. If it's winter, lace up and skate on the Pond, then get some hot chocolate in the concession area. Stop by the **Visitor's Center** for brochures and maps if you need them. If you are unfamiliar with the city, hop on an **Old Town Trolley Tour** to save time. You can hop on and off as time permits. Or, if you don't want to walk around, a **Boston Duck Tour** is a fun way to learn about the city. Pick a couple of sites you want to visit and explore them fully or just wander around **Beacon Hill**. Don't miss a ride on the **Swan Boats** in the **Public Garden** if it is warm out.

Why not start the next day with Sunday brunch at the **Museum of Science**? Afterwards, you can spend hours looking around the museum and maybe take in a movie at the IMAX or go to the observatory. Visit **Fanueil Hall** and **Quincy Market** for souvenirs and gifts, then eat at one of the many restaurants in the area.

Suggested Itineraries

Seven Days on Holiday

Begin with the "Whirlwind Weekend Tour" and then add the following. Spend one day in the **North End** and **Charlestown**. You can finish the **Freedom Trail** if you started it, exploring the USS *Constitution* and **Bunker Hill**. Stop in at **Paul Revere's House** and the **Old North Church**. Take a break at the **Langone Playground** right on the water and then eat somewhere in the **North End**. Finish the day with a children's show or a sporting event at the **FleetCenter**.

The next day, head down to the waterfront. Let your children take as much time as they want in the **Children's Museum**, then hop over to **the Boston Tea Party Ship & Museum**. Wander along the **HarborWalk** and end up at **Christopher Columbus Park** to play. Go to **Chinatown** for dinner.

On Day Five, begin at the **Mapparium** in the **Back Bay**, then head to the **Skywalk** at the Prudential for great views. Consider lunch in the Prudential Mall. Visit **Copley Square** and take a free tour of the **Boston Public Library**. See if there are any good half-price theatre tickets available at the **BosTix** in Copley Square while the kids play by the fountain and climb on the **Tortoise and Hare** statues. Walk down **Newbury Street**, then down to **Commonwealth Avenue**. You can stroll the **Commonwealth Mall** and stop for a playground break at the **Clarendon Street Playground** before deciding where to eat.

Take a whale watch, a harbor tour, or visit one of the harbor islands if you're here in season. Any visit to Boston is incomplete if you don't get out on the water. Alternatively, if it's cold, go to the **New England Aquarium** to see marine life up close. The 3D IMAX Theater is amazing here.

On your last day, visit **Harvard Square** in Cambridge. Count how many bookstores you see. Don't miss the **Curious George Goes to Wordsworth** bookstore. Take in the **Harvard Museums** and **Harvard Yard**, then hang out in the Square watching performers before you leave. Realize that you didn't touch on half of what Boston has to offer and start planning your next visit.

Chapter Seven

Island Getaways: Nantucket and Martha's Vineyard

Often mentioned in the same breath, Nantucket and Martha's Vineyard are two very different places, even when it comes down to their kid-friendliness. Though both islands can be visited as a day trip, it makes for a very long day, particularly for small children, so an overnight stay is in order. Two nights are best so you can have at least one leisurely day at the beach. The larger island inns are fine for children. I wouldn't recommend staying at a bed and breakfast except with older children. Generally, B&B guests are looking for peace and quiet. Also, antiques and kids aren't a good mix.

Getting There

You can drive or take a bus to where the ferries wait to take you across to either island, at various spots on Cape Cod, or you can fly. There are pricey commuter flights available from Boston's Logan International Airport as well as Hyannis, though most people (including me) take a ferry. It's pretty much a straight shot down Route 3 to the various ferry points There are two ferry services available and both have overnight parking facilities. Call the Steamship Authority ((508) 477-8600; **www.islandferry.com**), or Hy-Line Cruises ((800)492-8082; **www.hy-linecruises.com**). If you decide to take the bus, call Bonanza Bus Line ((800)556-3815; **www.bonazabus.com**) for times and prices.

Suggested Itineraries

Going to Nantucket

The Steamship Authority runs car ferries from Hyannis that take two hours and fifteen minutes to Nantucket Town. No reservations are required for passengers and bicycles. If you are planning on taking a car, however, you need to make reservations, in season, many months in advance. You can also just show up and play the odds at the standby queue, but this is not a sport for the faint of heart. The Hy-Line runs a high-speed passenger-only ferry from Hyannis that cuts the travel time down to an hour, but is more costly than Steamship Authority. They also run a two-hour conventional passenger ferry. Reservations are strongly recommended, particularly in the summer season.

Going to the Vineyard

The Steamship Authority ferry ride is only 45 minutes from Woods Hole to Vineyard Haven. In the summer, several boats a day run to Oak Bluffs instead of Vineyard Haven. If you have the choice, ride to Oak Bluffs. The Hy-Line runs only a conventional ferry from Hyannis to Vineyard Haven. The ride lasts an hour and thirty-five minutes.

Martha's Vineyard

Chamber of Commerce
Box 1698
Vineyard Haven, MA 02568
(508) 693-0085
www.mvy.com

Nobody is really quite sure where this large rural island got its name. The "Vineyard," as it is referred to by the initiated, can be easily seen in a day trip, but it only reveals its gentle charms when there is time to linger and explore. Though faced with the same conundrum of development versus preservation that confront all the last great places in the world, the Vineyard retains an unpolished, "just folks" rural character, which is a little bit deceiving. Spotting movie stars and other famous faces is a favorite tourist past time—many well-known people make their home here. The island is divided roughly into down-island and up-island.

Chapter Seven

Down-island towns:

Vineyard Haven, prudishly renamed so by Victorian sensibilities offended by the original moniker "Holmes Hole," is the main port of arrival for the ferries. Many island tour buses await day-trippers in the summertime and are well-worth the price if you need a quick guided overview of the island. There are also public transportation, rental car agencies, and bike rental shops right by the dock. Paved bike trails link the three down-island towns and also provide access to off-road trails in the State Forest, a large preserve that surrounds the airport in the center of the island. Near the ferry landing, a short stroll along the sand brings you to a small harbor beach and play-ground. There is a life-guard on duty in the summer. If you decide to walk along the shore, please note that in Massachusetts, property lines extend to the low tide line and some people have no tolerance for trespassers.

A view of the harbor.

Peter Simon Photography

Suggested Itineraries

When it's time to eat, head to the Black Dog Tavern (Beach Street Extension, (508) 693-9223). Though the thought of joining the hordes of people sporting the ubiquitous black lab silhouette T-shirts and sweatshirts may give you the willies, this Vineyard institution is quite good. The service is friendly, the waterfront location is beautiful, the ambiance is authentic, and the menu is inventive, eclectic, and kid-friendly. Though the waits tend to be long, the kids can run on the beach, stroll on the pier, and watch the ferries and boats come and go. The town is dry so BYOB. True story: One wintry day when we came to the island for the holiday festivals in December, my daughter didn't want to come in from playing in the snow. I made her. Tears ensued, but moments later our server showed up at the table with a gigantic bowl of snow, forever winning my gratitude.

Oak Bluffs: This town has its roots in religious revivals of the mid-19th century, when a huge tent would be set up and a town of tents would house worshippers who came in increasing numbers attracted in equal measure by piety and pleasure. Eventually the tents were replaced by Victorian gingerbread cottages that still give the campgrounds (as they are still called) a decidedly Disney-esque feel, except, this is the real thing. The Victorian architecture is everywhere in the town and makes for a charming tour. The town is also traditionally an African-American vacation spot dating back to the turn of the century, is home to the famous Inkwell Beach, and has the lion's share of the sites on the Vineyard's African American Heritage Trail.

Circuit Avenue (Oak Bluffs' main drag) and the harbor area are the closest that the Vineyard comes to the clamshack ambiance of mainland Cape Cod. Circuit Ave. is the best place to spot celebrities, so keep your eyes peeled for Carly Simon, Spike Lee, Dan Akroyd, and other celebrities (not that your kids will know who they are).

The Flying Horses carousel anchors one of the busiest intersections of the island and is a must for all children. This is the oldest operating

Chapter Seven

carousel in the nation: the beautiful, though sober, horses sport real horse-hair manes. Going for the brass ring to the sounds of the calliope will enchant the children and bring the adults back to a real or imagined childhood. As the town peters out when walking down Circuit Avenue, there is a good playground down Massasoit Avenue toward Waban Park.

There are several spots to eat. Try Offshore Ale (30 Kennebec Avenue; (508) 693-2626). The sawdust on the floor almost screams kid-friendly, and the barrel of roasted peanuts in their shells reinforces that thought. This microbrewery tavern offers a friendly atmosphere and a simple menu consisting of pub fare and pizzas. Linda Jean's Restaurant (34 Circuit Avenue; (508) 693-4093) is the quintessential diner, excellent for breakfast, and is what IHOP strives to be and fails. Fluffy pancakes smothered in fruit and other breakfast yummies.

Edgartown is the grande dame of the down-island towns that became rich in the 19th century (along with Nantucket) on whaling profits, and is still filled with the stately white, clapboarded federal-style mansions of the whaling captains. Definitely the tonier of the island towns, Main Street is filled with clothing and jewelry stores, restaurants and art galleries where Pissarros share exhibition space with local artists. The Harbor bustles in the summer season with sailboats of all sizes, and the fourth of July parade and fireworks is a preserved piece of Rockwellian Americana.

Right in Edgartown stands the Edgartown light that was recently turned into an understated and moving memorial to children taken from us before their time. I dare any parent to visit it and not at least feel the tears well up in their eyes. The walk to the light is beautiful and the right length, even for toddlers. A quiet harbor beach surrounds the light.

On the outskirts of town, just across from the cemetery, there is a small firefighting museum where children can play on a 1920s fire engine. For

Suggested Itineraries

better or worse, the engine features a hand-cranked, very loud siren. On a slow day, the firefighters may come over and invite you to bring the kids in to look at the working fire station with its ladder trucks and other rescue equipment. It is quite a treat and always rewarding to kids.

From Edgartown you can also take the ironically named "On Time" ferry (it leaves as soon as it is full and, hence, is by definition always 'on time'). It goes to the island of Chappaquidick. "Chappy" has some of the most beautiful beaches and nature walks on the islands. Our favorite for kids is the back harbor beach in the Wasque preserve—muddy flats that extend for miles with the water rarely reaching your knees. "Three-inch beach," as we have nicknamed it, is crowded only by horseshoe crabs, seagulls, terns and piping plovers, even in July and August. The adults can also walk over the dunes a few steps to access a beautiful Atlantic Ocean beach. Please note that there are no convenience stores at all in Chappy so make sure to bring along supplies, particularly water.

Peter Simon Photography

Gingerbread cottages charm kids and adults alike.

Chapter Seven

The Newes from America Pub (23 Kelly Street; (508) 627-4397) is a long-time favorite spot for lunch. Excellent pub fare and a good kid's menu are served in a down-to-earth atmosphere. One great place to stay with kids is the Colonial Inn in Edgartown ((800) 627-4701; www.colonialinn-mvy.com). This inn, built in 1912, is kid-friendly, with a library and games available for use. Some rooms have kitchenettes, so you can save on eating out. A complimentary breakfast is also offered and the views from the inn are spectacular. In season, a room with two double beds is around $250. There are dozens of places to stay on the Vineyard, but booking early is imperative. Visit the Chamber of Commerce's web page for listings.

Nantucket

Chamber of Commerce
48 Main Street
Nantucket, MA 02554
(508) 228-1700
www.nantucketchamber.org

Thirty miles out to sea from Hyannis, the "gray lady" is truly a land far away with its own unique beauty and a contrast from today's Cape Cod. Though it has recently been subjected to development pressure that is threatening to undermine its charm and character, the island is still filled with beautifully understated homes, open natural spaces, and unspoiled beaches. Nantucket is quite pricey, particularly as compared

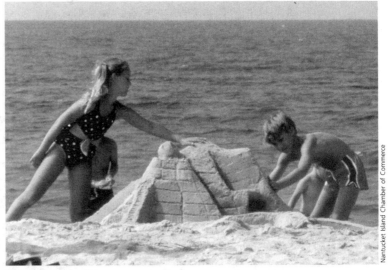

Building sand castles.

Nantucket Island Chamber of Commerce

Suggested Itineraries

to Martha's Vineyard; it costs more to get there, it's more expensive to stay, more expensive to eat, and is a very exclusive and upper-crust, old money destination where hundred-foot yachts are a common sight in summer.

If you did not bring a car, you will need a bike to use on the many miles of paved bike trails on the island. Renting a car is an expensive proposition, and the island is small enough and destinations are close enough, that you will have no problem without a car, even with kids in bike seats or towing trailers. There are several bike rental places in Nantucket town; however, I recommend Young's Bicycle at Steamboat Wharf, (617) 228-1151. The chief entertainment on the island is what you create yourself. A lazy day on the beach is as exciting as it gets. If your kids or you want a lot of excitement, you'd be better off on Martha's Vineyard.

In **Nantucket Town** federal-style homes, elegant understated restaurants, charming shops and art galleries on cobblestone streets invite window shopping and leisurely strolls—not something you will be doing if you have toddlers in tow (too bad). However, there is a harbor beach appropriately named "Children's Beach," an easy walk from town. It's ideal for small children and has a park with a new playground, game tables, and a bandstand. On the beach, there's a lifeguard, restrooms, showers, restaurant and take-out food service, and picnic tables. Restaurant, playground, and rest room are all wheelchair-accessible. Other beaches appropriate for children include Dionis and Jetties beaches, both easily accessible by bike trail.

The Nantucket Maria Mitchell Association (4 Vestal Street; (508) 228-9198; **www.mmo.org**) runs a small aquarium, an observatory, a natural science museum, and operates weeklong camps and day activities in season for children of all ages.

Chapter Seven

Food just tastes better in Nantucket, and there is a definite island style. Here are a couple of recommendations for kid-friendly places:

The Brotherhood of Thieves (23 Broad Street). Burgers, specialty sandwiches, and soups; wonderful, friendly atmosphere, music some nights. Careful though—they don't take credit cards.

Cap'n Tobey's Chowder House (Straight Wharf; (508) 228-0836). A Nantucket institution, chowder, fresh seafood and an extensive children's menu.

Brant Point Grill at the White Elephant (50 Easton St.; (800) 475-2637; **www.whiteelephanthotel.com**). For a wonderful al fresco lunch, you can't beat the terrace at the White Elephant, where you can watch the sailboats drift by in the harbor. Lots of room for the kids to roam. This is also one of the best places to stay with kids on the island. For more accommodations options, call the Chamber of Commerce.

8

Appendices

Freebies
Calendar of Events
Helpful Numbers & Websites

Appendix A

Tips, Freebies & Restrooms

This is an obvious one, but try to visit tourist-heavy sites during the week. There is no real non-tourist season in Boston and weekends find tourists, and natives, out in droves no matter what time of year it is. Weekdays are a bit less crowded.

Go during lunchtime if you can. Decide if you can eat early, or late, and bring snacks and water. Not everyone else will have thought of this, so while they are waiting in long concession lines, you'll have a little more room to breathe. And you'll save money while you're at it. Food is never cheap at a museum.

Do your homework. Read the next section on freebies and find out how to get bargains. No one is going to volunteer that there are often two-for-one tickets or specials deals available. You have to ask. It's a bummer to find out that if you had just come the day before or waited a couple of hours, your visit could have been free or discounted.

And that brings us to bargains. It's not cheap to travel, especially in Boston. If you can do a little extra legwork and schedule carefully, there are all sorts of deals to be had here in Beantown. Bostonians are notoriously frugal, so you'll have the added bonus of doing as the natives do.

Here are a few pointers, but these may change at any time. If you can, call or visit the website of every place you think you might visit to see what their latest deals are. At the very least, call the Boston Tourist Board to get their tourist information. You can also order a useful guide from the tourist board, called "Kids Love Boston" geared for children. It has fun facts and games inside. (Call (888) SEE-BOSTON.)

TIP FOR LOCALS: All you need is a Boston Public Library card and a little foresight to get free or discounted tickets to many local museums. Every library gets a certain amount of tickets from various institutions for many venues around town, including the Children's Museum, the Museum of Fine Arts, and the Harvard Museums. Call your local library to see what they have. You can reserve the tickets with your card. For example, a Children's Museum pass, good for six people, reduces the entry to just $2 per person.

These venues have free or discounted entry fees on certain days.

Museum of Fine Arts: Free admission on Wednesday after 4 p.m. (contribution voluntary); on Thursdays and Fridays after 5 p.m., get $2 off tickets. All tickets are good for two days.

Harvard Museums: Free admission on Sunday, 9 a.m. - noon; Wednesday from 3-5 p.m.

Children's Museum: Fridays, $1 admission after 5 p.m.

Franklin Park Zoo: Free admission until noon, first Saturday of the month.

Tips, Freebies & Restrooms

More Discounts & Deals

Call or visit to buy advance or discount tickets to all sorts of venues in the city at the following places.

Arts/Mail & Arts/Boston Coupon Book

325 Columbus Avenue, Suite 11
Boston, MA 02116
(800) ARTS-MAIL; fax (617) 262-8633
www.artsboston.org

Add your name to the mailing list to get a free mail order guide to Boston events. Huge discounts abound in the guide, and you can order in advance. In general, fees for events are half-price. There is a service charge.

The Arts/Boston coupon book costs $9 and has great 2-for-1 offers to museums such as the Children's Museum and the Museum of Science. Dozens of attractions have coupons in the book, including trolley tours and even sights out of town.

BosTix

(617) 482-BTIX
BosTix booths: Copley Square & Faneuil Hall Marketplace
www.boston.com/artsboston

If you can be flexible, this is a great way to save money. BosTix sells half-price, day-of-the-show tickets to all sorts of arts events around town. They also sell full-price advance tickets and serve as a Ticketmaster outlet. They accept cash only.

Appendix A

Boston CityPass

Call (707) 256-0490
www.citypass.com

Boston CityPass

Cost: adult, $25.25, children 3-17, $16.

This pass is good for the following five attractions in the city: Museum of Science, Museum of Fine Arts, Boston, New England Aquarium, John F. Kennedy Library and Museum, and the Harvard Museum of Natural History. It's a great idea for those on a serious sightseeing trip. You can buy the pass at any of the attractions. It's good for nine days, starting from the day you buy it. You not only save 50% off ticket prices, but once you buy the pass, you can skip the ticket lines at the rest of the sites you visit.

MBTA Visitor's Passport

You can buy an unlimited travel pass for one day ($6); three days, ($11); or seven days ($22). This pass is good for train and bus service. Call the MBTA at (617) 222-3200 for more info or to order your passes in advance, or you can visit their visit their website at **www.mbta.com**.

I Gotta Go!

It's always a good idea to scout out bathrooms when traveling around. I try to find the nearest bookstore and, fortunately, Boston is filled with bookstores. Many of them even have bathrooms right in the children's section complete with diaper-changing stations. Libraries are usually my next choice. All towns have one, and they can't tell you no. Believe it or not, there's a whole section dedicated to public restrooms, with a user's rating scale, at **www.boston-online.com/restrooms**. Hotels seem to top the list, followed by malls and restaurants.

Calendar of Events

Appendix B

Calendar of Events

January

Annual New Year's Day swim
Join or watch the L Street Swimming Club Brownies in their traditional dip in South Boston. (617) 635-5104.

Japanese New Year
Celebrate at the Children's Museum. Arts & crafts, demonstrations, music and more. (617) 451-0726.

February

Chinese New Year
(617) 635-3485

March

New England Spring Flower Show
Remind yourself spring is coming at the annual flower show at the Bayside Exposition Center. (617) 536-9280.

St. Patrick's Day Parade/Evacuation Day (Massachusetts holiday)
(617) 536-4100.

April

Patriot's Day/Boston Marathon
The oldest marathon in the U.S. Finish line in Copley Square. (617) 236-1652; **www.bostonmarathon.com**. Patriot's Day parade leaves from City Hall at 9:30 a.m. followed by reenactment of Paul Revere's ride. (617) 635-4447.

Swan Boats Return to Public Garden
Celebrate the arrival of Spring with the return of the Swan Boats.

Appendix B

May

Lilac Sunday (Mother's Day)
View 250 different blooms at Arnold Arboretum. (617) 524-1718.

Make Way for Ducklings Parade
(Mother's Day) Register at noon at Boston Common to march like a duck. (617) 426-1885.

Kite Festival
Make, fly, or just watch at Franklin Park. (617) 635-4505.

June

Art in the Park Festival (DeCordova Museum)
Activities for children, music, entertainment. (781) 259-8355.

Bunker Hill Day (Boston holiday)
Re-enactments, parade. (617) 242-5628.

Concerts at the Hatch Shell
Come hear music or see a performance. (617) 727-5251.

Dragon Boat Festival
Beautifully decorated boats race on the Charles. (617) 426-6500, ext. 778, www.bostondragonboat.org

Scooper Bowl
Delicious ice cream fundraiser. 800-52JIMMY.

Free Friday Flicks at the Hatch Shell
(617) 727-5114, ext.530; www.state.ma.us/mdc.

Calendar of Events

July

Boston Pops Fourth of July Concert
At the Hatchshell. (617) 266-1492.

Chowderfest
Gorge on chowder at this July 4th tradition at City Hall Plaza. (617) 227-1528; **www.bostonharborfest.com/chowderfest/**.

Harborfest
Boston celebrates the waterfront with events through the week. (617) 227-1528. **www.bostonharborfest.com**

North End Italian Festivals
Celebrating saints with feasts and parades. (617) 536-4100.

August

August Moon Festival
Chinatown festival. Parade, music, and food. (617) 542-2574.

North End Italian Feasts
Celebrate the saints all summer. (617) 635-3911.

September

The Big E
The Eastern States Exposition in Springfield, MA, has agricultural events, amusement rides, music, parades, and more. (800) 334-BIGE; **www.thebige.com**.

Appendix B

October

Head of the Charles Regatta
Racing on the Charles River. (617) 864-8415; www.hocr.org.

Lantern Festival
Dusk festival at Jamaica Pond.

November

Veteran's Day Parade
The 1 p.m. parade kicks off in the Back Bay. (617) 635-3911.

Boston Ballet's Nutcracker
The annual favorite at the Wang Center. (800) 447-7400;
www.bostonballet.org.

Enchanted Village
Visit an animated re-creation of a turn-of-the-century village on a snowy
Christmas Eve at City Hall Plaza. (617) 635-3689.

Teddy Bear Tea
Do good and have fun at the annual Teddy Bear Tea at the Omni Parker
House, a charity event to benefit needy children. (978) 356-2602.
www.teddybeardrive.org.

Holiday Lighting Ceremony
Kick off the season at Faneuil Hall's Lighting Ceremony. Performances
and food all day. Lights come on at 5 p.m. (617) 523-1300.
www.faneuilhallmarketplace.com.

Boston Common Frog Pond
The pond opens up for ice-skating. (617) 635-2120.

Calendar of Events

December

Winter Wonderland Train Display
Check out the 400 feet of track laid out at South Station. Little villages, bridges, and tunnels make a charming scene.

Tree Lightings
The two biggies are the Prudential Holiday Tree Lighting and the Boston Common Holiday Lighting the first weekend of this month. **www.bostonusa.com**.

Christmas Revels
Winter Solstice celebration at Harvard's Sanders Theatre. Every year features a different theme. (617) 469-2222.

First Night
New Year's Eve celebration for everyone, with more than 250 events throughout the city. Buy a button to gain admission to all the festivities in dozens of venues. (617) 542-1399; **www.firstnight.org**.

Appendix C

Appendix C

Helpful Numbers & Websites

Greater Boston Convention & Visitors Bureau

2 Copley Place, Suite 105
Boston, MA 02116
(617) 536-4100; 888-SEE-BOSTON
www.bostonusa.com

One-stop shopping for information on everything Boston. Very helpful site helps you plan your trip with tips, prices, and more. Links to other websites make it easy to figure out what you want to do. Go to the Family Friendly Values section for special deals.

Boston and Massachusetts websites

www.cityofboston.com/calendar/calendar.asp

A great website to find out what's going on when you are visiting. Recurring and one-day events are listed. You can search by neighborhood, date, or event.

Boston-Online

www.boston-online.com

Another useful site with links to all sorts of Boston stuff, including where to find public bathrooms and Boston etiquette. It's a humorous but accurate site that doesn't take itself seriously. It offers little-known facts about Beantown.

Helpful Numbers & Websites

Cambridge Office for Tourism

4 Brattle Street, Suite 208
Cambridge, MA 02138
(617) 441-2884; (800) 862-5678
www.cambridge-usa.org

Destination Plymouth

225 Water Street, Suite 202
Plymouth, MA 02360
(508) 747-7533; (800) USA-1620
www.visit-plymouth.com

Destination Salem

59 Wharf Street, Suite C-2
Salem, MA 01970
(978) 744-3663; 877-SALEMMA
www.salem.org

GoCityKids

www.gocitykids.com

This fabulous website has the lowdown on everything to do around Boston with children complete with a daily calendar. Check it out for the days you are visiting to see what's going on. You can sign up for a newsletter updating you on events.

Appendix C

Greater Merrimack Valley Convention & Visitors Bureau

9 Central St., Suite 201
Lowell, MA 01852
(800) 433-3332; 978-459-6150
www.lexington-concord.org

Covers Lexington, Concord, and Lowell.

Mass Vacations

www.massvacations.com

Make reservations for hotels, B & Bs, and inns.

MBTA

(617) 722-3200; www.mbta.com

Nantucket Island Chamber of Commerce

48 Main Street
Nantucket, MA 02554
(508) 228-0659;
www.nantucketchamber.org

Martha's Vineyard Chamber of Commerce

Box 1698
Vineyard Haven, MA 02568
(508) 693-0085
www.mvy.com

8

Index

175

parent's guide press

Good For You.
Good For Your Kids.

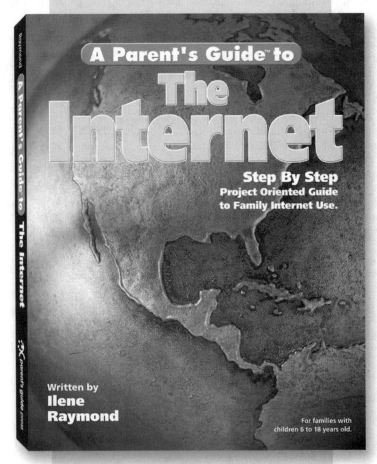

A Parent's Guide to THE INTERNET
ISBN 0-9675127-9-4
$19.95 (December 2001)

208 Pages —Trade Paperback—Available in Library Bindings
Hundreds of Website Listings, Dozens of Illustrations, Index

The only book about kids and the Internet to be published in the last two years.

"(An) imaginative, valuable resource"

—American Library Association

• **HTML explained.** How building a family Web site helps parents and children better understand the Internet (and have fun at the same time).

• **A brief history of the Internet** (and why the Internet is more than the World Wide Web and vice versa).

• **E-mail, Discussion Groups, FTP, IRC Chat**: the Internet that isn't the Web and the opportunities for enlightenment— and abuse— they offer.

• **Advice from experts** such as Slashdot columnist Jon Katz, MaMaMedia.com founder Idit Harel, researcher Michael Antecol and many others: Internet developers, child psychology experts, homeschooling parents, academics, and involved educators. All share insights on how best to use the Internet in the home. In short: Parents need to be involved with their children's Internet activity. The Internet is not a teacher, parent, sibling, babysitter or friend, though it is a powerful communication medium that can help children, grow, learn, meet, and explore.

• **Scores of Web sites** to explore and enjoy, from games to filtering services, online encyclopedias to blogs.

• **A concise glossary** of common Internet and computer terms makes the jargon comprehensible.

• **Indexed** for easy reference.

• **The project oriented non-technical guide to family Internet use.** Dozens of hands-on projects for parents and children help de-mystify the Internet and lay bare issues of privacy, youth-targeted marketing, and safety.

• **Written by Ilene Raymond**, an award winning writer and essayist who has taught at Temple University and Pennsylvania State University. Her articles and fiction have appeared in numerous national publications, including Good Housekeeping, Redbook, Cosmopolitan, Readers Digest, Ladies House Journal, and Mademoiselle. She lives outside Philadelphia with her husband and two sons.